MORE THAN WORDS

MORE THAN WORDS

Revised Edition

A Resource Book for Church School Teachers and for Students in Junior High School Classes

Materials for Christian Education
Prepared at the Direction of General Convention

THE SEABURY PRESS
NEW YORK

More Than Words was prepared by the Department of Christian Education of the National Council of the Protestant Episcopal Church at the direction of General Convention as part of the Church's Teaching for closely graded church schools.

Library of Congress Catalogue Card Number: 58-9264

Scriptural quotations, unless taken from the Book of Common Prayer, are from the *Revised Standard Version of the Bible,* copyright 1946 and 1952 by the Division of Christian Education, National Council of Churches.

THIRD PRINTING, 1963
275-663-LP-65-35
PRINTED IN THE UNITED STATES OF AMERICA

PREFACE

EVERY FIELD OF STUDY AND PLEASURE has its own technical language. There is a language of machines, a language of sailing, a language of sewing, and a language of music. We learn to "talk terms" as we learn to play the game.

When we are about to be confirmed, we begin to use the language of the Episcopal Church. We could not think very much about religion if we did not understand the words in which important ideas are expressed. This book was written to help you understand words you will hear and words you will need to use.

In a number of cases where a word has several meanings, *More Than Words* takes up only those which are the most important, or the most usual, or the most likely to stand for something which you have met in your own life. The other meanings can be found by following the index to THE CHURCH'S TEACHING on page 205. In addition to many quotations from the Bible, special passages from the Book of Common Prayer are mentioned. It will help you to look them up. Hymns are suggested which show how the words are used. Some of them are your favorites.

As you work with this book, you will find that part of every article is every *other* article mentioned in the cross references. The editors tried to make each article short enough to be read quickly. Instead of repeating ideas expressed somewhere else in the book, they have directed you to all the other places that will give you additional understanding.

The truth of the Christian faith is so rich and meaningful that it is impossible to express it all in any one book. It is even impossible for any one person to understand it all or to express what he believes in such a way that everyone else will agree with him. We have differences of opinion within our Episcopal Church, but by talking over those differences we learn from each other and move a little nearer eternal truth. This book makes no effort to convince anyone on any of the lesser points about which Churchmen differ. Its purpose is to present clearly the important things on which we agree.

MORE THAN WORDS

A

ABSOLUTION
means setting free from sin

FOR A MEMBER of the Church absolution means God's pardon spoken by a priest. (You will understand this better if you first look up "forgiveness.") God loves me. Even if I have been very bad, He still loves me and wants to forgive me. He doesn't say, "I will forgive you *if* you pay back, or *if* you are good from now on." He just forgives as soon as I am willing to accept His forgiveness and be His friend. No matter how bad my sin was, He will forgive me as soon as I really trust Him.

But forgiveness is not just a private deal between God and me. My sins have built invisible walls between me and other people. And I very much need to be in a family of people who accept me and understand me. So, when I was baptized I was reborn into the family of Christ's Church. And if I sin after baptism I may be brought back into the Family again. The words the priest uses to bring me back are called "absolution." When he says them he is speaking for God and for all of God's people. God and His Church are taking me back.

Absolution is something *like* what happens at home when a member of the family "goes away mad" and Mother succeeds in bringing him back. When Mother puts an arm around him and forgives him, she is doing it, not just for herself, but for the whole family. She says the words, but the whole family forgives him. In God's family, God lets His priest say the words, but the forgiveness comes from God and from His Church.

The Church helps us ask for absolution. In our private prayers we think of the wrong things we have done and tell them to God. Then when we go to church, we join our fellow Christians in saying the General Confession. We ask God to forgive all of us and free us from our sins. The priest says that God pardons and absolves all who intend to change their ways and trust God.

The priest's words are spoken to a whole congregation. One reason for this is that some sins are the fault of the whole group. If your town still has an awful slum, that isn't any one person's fault, but everybody's together. If strangers or people of other races come to church and nobody speaks to them, we all need to be forgiven. So we confess all together and all together receive forgiveness.

Sometimes a person goes to his minister for help when he is troubled about his sins. He and the minister talk over his problems and seek help, ending with a prayer for absolution. Church people may also confess their sins privately in the presence of a priest. The priest declares to the person who is penitent that God gives him absolution. By this the person is restored to fellowship.

Suggestions for further reading

The Hymnal: 435.

4

The Book of Common Prayer: The Declaration of Absolution on page 7 and other forms on pages 24, 76, and 323. The Exortation, pages 86–88, especially the last paragraph.

Other articles: Atonement, Confession, Conscience, Forgiveness, Penitence, Separation, Sin.

Questions

What do the words *miserable offenders* mean in the General Confession? What is meant by "Forgive us our trespasses, as we forgive those who trespass against us"?

ACCEPTANCE
means letting a person know he is wanted

WE LIKE SOME PEOPLE and dislike others. We feel this way about groups as well as individuals. Someone may seem strange to us when we meet him, and someone whom we like at one time may change and be unpleasant at another. But every person is always just as much a child of God as every other person.

A member of the Church tries to recognize the needs of other people. One of their needs is to be accepted *as they are*. I can't say to the people who annoy me, "I want you to change to suit me." Maybe if I take them as they are, make them feel welcome and liked, they will change a little. Maybe I'll change a little, too!

When I feel welcomed and liked, I can be my very best self. I can come nearer to being the likable person I want to be. So if I make other people feel truly wanted and appreciated, they too can feel more at ease with me and begin really to *be* likable.

We can accept—or feel accepted—through very small words and actions: a greeting, a look, a smile, a slight touch of the hand, the simple act of moving over to make room, or sharing food and drink. All of these things say, "You're one of us." I may be the only one who does it, but if I reach out to a new or friendless person, my crowd will be more likely to take him in, too.

For us the hardest thing may be to accept a person who has hurt us or who does not seem to want us as a friend. God, in Jesus Christ, made it possible for us to do this. For God accepts us as we are and everyone else as he is. Because God accepts us, we find it easier to accept other people.

Making a person welcome and at ease with us is one of the most important things we can do as Christians. We can't do it without God's help, but when God helps us accept another person, that person knows the love of God as it comes to him through us.

Suggestions for further reading

The Hymnal: 493.
The Book of Common Prayer: The story on page 208.
Other articles: Forgiveness, Grace, Justification by Faith, Love.

Questions

Is a Christian expected to like everybody? Are there differences between *liking* and *accepting?*

ADULTERY

means breaking the solemn promise a man and woman
make to each other when they marry

WHEN CHURCH PEOPLE MARRY, they solemnly promise before God to live together as husband and wife, to love and honor each other as long as both of them live, "forsaking all others." They freely give themselves to each other. Marriage is built on a promise which both partners intend to keep. If either one breaks this promise by having sexual intercourse with another person, that is adultery. The word can be used also to describe any situation where either partner to a marriage transfers his affection and loyalty to someone else and thus breaks the holy marriage vows. This means, of course, being disloyal, and it severely hurts and damages the love which drew the husband and wife together in the first place.

Jesus said, "But from the beginning of creation, 'God made them male and female.' 'For this reason a man shall leave his father and mother and be joined to his wife, and the two shall become one.' So they are no longer two but one. What therefore God has joined together, let not man put asunder." (Mark 10:6–9) Adultery separates what God has joined.

Suggestions for further reading

The Book of Common Prayer: The Marriage Service, pages 300–304.

Questions

What makes a marriage stick? What movies have you ever seen that give a true picture of marriage?

7

ADVENT

*is the season that begins on the fourth Sunday
before Christmas and ends on Christmas Eve*

THE WORD *advent* means "coming," and refers to the
coming of Jesus Christ which we celebrate on Christmas
Day. The First Sunday in Advent is the Christian New
Year's Day. During the Church seasons, beginning with
Advent, we remember the great events of Christ's earthly
life, and in our imagination we relive them. We make a
sort of drama of them as if they were acts and scenes in
a sacred play.

Advent, like Lent, is a season of preparation. During
Advent we prepare our hearts and minds for Christmas
by saying HE IS COMING!! We want to make sure that on
Christmas Day the spirit of Jesus Christ is "born anew" in
our hearts.

The season of Advent says that Christ has come, that
He is still coming, and that He will come again to judge
all things. He came in Jesus, He comes to us in the life
of the Church, and He is the final Judge of all that we do.

Suggestions for further reading

The Book of Common Prayer: page 90.
The Hymnal: 235.
Other articles: Judgment, Second Coming.

Questions

What should we do during Advent to prepare for the
Christmas feast in a Christian way?

ALMIGHTY
refers to the ruling power of God

ONE OF THE BIBLE'S NAMES for God is "the Almighty" or "Almighty God." This means that all the power there is comes from God. God rules what He has made. In the long run nothing can defeat Him. He is the Sovereign Ruler. He is entirely able to do all the good things He sets out to do. He cannot and will not do evil or anything else that contradicts His love. He can do and does everything that is true, just, and loving.

God's love is powerful, and nothing can destroy it. It will outlast everything else. In Jesus we see God's love. Jesus cared about all kinds of people. Men turned their backs on Him, but when Jesus was crucified, He prayed for their forgiveness. Here was love that nothing could overcome. From all that Jesus said and did, we know that nothing is more powerful than God's love. "For I am sure that neither death, nor life, . . . nor anything else in all creation, will be able to separate us from the love of God in Christ Jesus our Lord." (Rom. 8:38–39)

Suggestions for further reading

The Hymnal: 279, 538.
Other articles: Creation, Cross, God, Judgment, Love.

Questions

Give some illustrations of the way God's power works for good. How do you think Christians can use "bad breaks" to further God's purpose?

AMEN
means "I agree"

WHEN SAID AFTER A PRAYER, *Amen* means "This is what I want," or "This is how I feel," or "So be it!" After a statement of belief, it means "This is what I really believe." In our Lord's time it was also used before an important saying to warn the people to listen. In translating "Amen" the King James Version of the Bible uses *verily*, which means "truly," or sometimes "Listen carefully to what I say to you."

Suggestions for further reading

The Hymnal: 279 (stanza 4).

Questions

In services in the Episcopal Church, why does the whole congregation say "Amen" after each prayer? In the Book of Common Prayer, what is the difference between an "Amen" in italics and one in regular type?

ANGELS
are God's messengers, who praise Him in heaven and assist us on earth

IN THE SERVICE OF Holy Communion we hear the words: "Therefore with Angels and Archangels, and with all the company of heaven, we laud and magnify thy glorious Name." This wonderful language means that in our praise and worship of God we are united with a great company of unseen friends who are always worshiping and serving God.

We read in the Bible that angels speak to Gideon and to Elijah and to many others. In the Old Testament, the word *angel* is sometimes used to refer to an appearance of God. At other times an angel is a heavenly messenger who serves God. Later, the Jews thought of angels as bringers of help from God to men. In the New Testament the angel Gabriel reveals God's will to Mary; a host of angels appear to the shepherds in the Christmas story; angels speak to St. Peter and to St. Philip; angels will be present on Judgment Day.

The Bible makes it plain to us all that God has messengers and helpers besides human people. These heavenly messengers still "speak" to us in a spiritual fashion, warning us of evil and encouraging us to do good. Through them, God cares for us and seeks to help and guide us.

Suggestions for further reading

The Hymnal: 42, 600.
The Book of Common Prayer: pages 251–252.
Other articles: Devil.

Questions

Why do artists often picture angels as having wings? Why do we not become angels after death?

AN APOSTLE
is one who is sent forth by Christ

AN APOSTLE IS SENT with authority. He is given a message to carry to someone else. Today when an ambassador is appointed and sent to some foreign country by the President, he speaks and acts with the authority which has been given him.

In the New Testament we read that our Lord chose twelve men to be with Him. Later He sent them out to preach the Good News of the Kingdom, to drive out demons, and to heal. The twelve whom Jesus chose came to be called *apostles*. They had been given authority and power to act for Jesus and for His Church. They had learned from Jesus; they had shared His life and seen His work; they were witnesses of His resurrection.

The writers of the first three Gospels, (St. Matthew, St. Mark, and St. Luke) give us slightly different lists of the twelve men appointed by Jesus. St. John mentions only eight by name.

Judas Iscariot, who betrayed Jesus, committed suicide. When the remaining eleven met after the first Easter, they chose a twelfth man, Matthias, to take Judas Iscariot's place. See Acts 1:15–26. This story gives the qualifications for an apostle. He must have been a witness to the Resurrection. Later on, Paul, Barnabas, and others were considered apostles. (Acts 13:1–3) Today our bishops perform the functions of the apostles.

There is a difference between an apostle and a disciple. A disciple is loyal to a teacher and learns what he is taught. An apostle has Christ's authority to teach and to act for Him. The risen Christ appeared to the eleven and said, "Go therefore and make disciples of all nations, baptizing them in the name of the Father and of the Son and of the Holy Spirit, teaching them to observe all that I have commanded you; and lo, I am with you always, to the close of the age." (Matt. 28:19–20)

Suggestions for further reading

Other articles: Bishop, Confirmation, Disciple, Mission, Witness.

Questions

Why is a Christian missionary like both a disciple and an apostle? Why do you think it was necessary that an apostle be one who knew that Jesus Christ had risen from the dead?

THE ASCENSION

*marks the triumph of Jesus Christ
and His continual presence with us*

ON THE FIRST EASTER MORNING God raised Jesus from death. After that, Christ showed Himself to His apostles many times. The last time He showed Himself was the Ascension. The apostles believed that Jesus went to a place beyond the sky. Many people today would not use such terms. We know more about the sun, moon, planets, and space than the apostles did. After the Ascension the apostles had to know our Lord in a new way, which is the way we know Him today. Through prayer, the fellowship of the Holy Spirit, and the Church's worship we know that He is with us. In the Holy Communion He gives us His presence in a real and special way.

The fact of the Ascension assures us that Christ was triumphant and was given the highest place of power and authority. It also assures us that Jesus ascended to heaven with our human experience part of His own. Thus He is our Mediator and Intercessor because in His human nature He knows our needs.

In His earthly life Jesus could be in only one place at a time. The Ascension made it possible for us to find the living Christ wherever we may be—on land, at sea, in the air.

Suggestions for further reading

The Hymnal: 103, 354.
The Book of Common Prayer: pages 177–178.
Other articles: Heaven, Hell, Mediator, Resurrection.

ATONEMENT
*means the healing or mending of a hurt
or broken relationship*

WHEN YOU AND A GOOD FRIEND have a quarrel, you sometimes feel more like enemies than friends. Often, however, you succeed in being happy together again, and then you understand each other even better than before. The words *at one* make the word *atone*, so that *atonement* really means "at-one-ment" or "being made at one."

In the Christian religion the Atonement is what God did when Jesus Christ brought men back into oneness with Himself. In the human life of Jesus, by His death and resurrection, God made us "at one" with Him. Thus St. Paul says "God was in Christ reconciling the world to himself." (II Cor. 5:19)

In the Atonement, God in Christ made it possible for men and women and children to be in harmony with Him

14

in spite of the fact that we are undeserving. The Atonement could only have been the work of God, a gift made by Him who is Love.

Only God can rescue us from our sins. We are powerless, caught in the trap of our self-will. But the rescue is not complete until we trust Him.

Suggestions for further reading

The Hymnal: 68.

Other articles: Absolution, Calvary, Cross, Forgiveness, Incarnation, Mediator, Reconciliation, Redemption, Saviour.

Questions

When you have had a falling out with your parents, how can the relationship be restored? Explain how our relationship with God is like this.

AUTHORITY
means rightful power, the right to command or to act

WHEN A POLICEMAN BLOWS HIS WHISTLE at an intersection, we respect his authority by obeying his signals. When a good teacher explains an idea in class, he knows what he's talking about. When our parents tell us that we have to come in at a particular time, or when they give us some chore to do at home, we may not always be happy about it, but we understand that they have the right to do this because they are our parents.

When a person knows what he is doing and has the right to do it, we recognize that he has authority.

If boys are going to play a game of softball without spending all their time arguing, they have to respect the rules of game. There is nothing to stop them from inventing a game with new rules if they want to, but they should not call it softball.

In the same way, the Church has the right to teach the Christian religion. The Church has the right to interpret the teachings of the Bible. The Church has the right to set the patterns for worship. If we are going to be serious Christians, we must respect this authority. We can think for ourselves, but our judgments are double checked by the higher authority of the Church.

Suggestions for further reading

The Hymnal: 301.
Other articles: Almighty, Conscience, Law, Obey.

Questions

When are *you* in a position of authority? Why are you given this authority? What does the Book of Common Prayer say about submitting to authority? (See page 288.)

B

BAPTISM
*is the sacrament by which a person becomes
a member of the Church*

BAPTISM MAKES YOU A MEMBER of the family of God, the Church, forever. Of course God has created and loves all His children. But by water and "in the Name of the Father, and of the Son, and of the Holy Ghost," the Church receives you not just as "a" child but as "the" child of God.

There are two ways of coming into a family: being born and being adopted. God adopted you into His family when you were baptized. Jesus is God's son. All the rest of us are adopted. When God adopts us, He doesn't just make us welcome. He puts a *new life* into us. Because of that new life we are "regenerated"; that is, we are born again.

Every family has a "spirit" all its own. In God's family the spirit is God the Holy Spirit who is given us in baptism.

But the Church is more than just a family: it is a living body—the Body of Christ. You and I belong to Christ, not just as relatives, but in the way your hand or foot belongs to you. Christ can use us as you can use your hand, and just as your hand gets blood from you to keep it alive, so we keep getting life from our Lord. Because this process begins when we are baptized, we say that in baptism we become *members of Christ*. As members we have responsibilities and privileges. "The Church is the Body of which Jesus Christ is the Head, and all baptized people are the members." (Prayer Book, page 290)

Your godparents have promised *for you* that you will:

1. Turn your back on unchristian thoughts and words and acts. (This is what the Book of Common Prayer means by "renounce the devil and all his works, the vain pomp and glory of the world, with all covetous desires of the same, and the sinful desires of the flesh.")

2. Believe all the teachings of the Christian faith as found in the Apostles' Creed.

3. Keep God's commandments, with His help.

Your godparents have promised *for themselves* to see to it that you learn the things a Christian ought to know and believe, and that you will be confirmed and so become a responsible, grown-up member of the Church. It is the duty of godparents to see that the parish church school helps them to carry out their duties.

When you are confirmed, you renew and take over the promises made at your Baptism, and you are strengthened by God the Holy Spirit to do this.

Suggestions for further reading

The Book of Common Prayer: pages 273–282, 283.

Other articles: Church, Confirmation, Godparents, Holy Spirit, Inheritor, Name, Sacrament.

Questions

How does baptism differ for a child and an adult? (Book of Common Prayer, pages 276–278) What does a person do if he doesn't know whether or not he has been baptized? (Page 282) Why does the Episcopal Church usually baptize people in infancy?

BELIEF

*is confidence that something is true
or that it is reliable*

WHEN THE TEMPERATURE IS BELOW FREEZING and I put a pan of water out-of-doors, I believe the water will become ice. I may believe that my dog can run faster than your dog, and we may be able to arrange a race to prove it. Beliefs like this can be tested by the facts.

We also have confidence that *some* things are true even when we cannot prove them. No one of us has ever seen God, but we still believe that God *is*.

Belief also has another meaning. It means to trust someone or something as reliable. I believe *in* my parents. They care about me, and I can count on them to love me even when I have done things that hurt them.

The Creed begins, "I believe *in* God the Father Almighty." This means that I trust God, who runs the universe. What I do is important not only to me but also to God. I believe *in* Jesus Christ. When I trust Him, I can make choices and act in obedience to His truth. I believe *in* the Holy Spirit, who strengthens me to grow into the kind of person I ought to be.

Suggestions for further reading

The Hymnal: 330.
Other articles: Creed, Faith, Religion, Right.

Questions

What are some things that you believe strongly? Whom do you believe *in?*

THE BIBLE
*is the book which tells us how our religion
came to us and what it is*

CHRISTIANITY IS a historical religion. That is, it came to us through the experience of actual people. The Bible is the story of how God guided the things that happened to the Israelites and later to those who knew Jesus and those who were his followers. It is all about people and what happens to them because God is at work in His world and in Christ. Yet the Bible is first of all a book about God—He is the "hero."

The Church believes that the people who wrote the Bible were so inspired that these books are the most important collection in the world. That is why we reverence the Bible and give it a place of honor on the lectern in church. That is why we read from it at every service.

The Bible was written by many people who lived in many different centuries. The word *bible* really means a collection of books, a small library. It is made up of sixty-six books, some of them very short. They are of many different kinds and include religious history, poetry, sermons, romances, hymns, prayers, laws, and letters.

All the Bible stories have meaning for our lives because we are part of God's people. But to tell the good news about Jesus Christ a *new* kind of writing had to be invented. We find this new form in the four Gospels.

All the Church's teaching is based on the Bible. Every ordained minister has to promise not to ask anyone to believe or do anything which the Bible does not support. Most of the Book of Common Prayer comes straight from the Bible, including the words in many of the prayers. Because the Bible tells us God's laws and gives us the Gospel of Christ and shows how God made himself known, we call it the Word of God.

The Bible has two parts, the Old Testament (or Covenant) and the New. The Old Testament is the sacred book of the Jews as well as part of the Christian sacred scriptures. It was the Bible Jesus used. The New Testament contains the writings which came into being and became precious to the Christian Church during the first three generations after the Resurrection. It is the only place where we can read what those who knew Jesus wrote about Him. The Old Testament was written in Hebrew and the New Testament in Greek, so that the Bible in English, or in any other modern language, is a *translation*.

Because it was written in ancient times by so many different people, the Bible is hard to understand. It is therefore necessary to have classes and study groups led by people who have learned how to use the Bible. One guide for us in learning what the Bible says is to read the psalms and lessons listed in the Prayer Book on pages ix–xlv, and the Epistles and Gospels on pages 90–269. Many Christians find it a help to read a part of the Bible every day.

Since we can guide our lives by the Bible it has been

called a "Light" or a "Compass" (Hymns 400, 402), as well as the "Book of Books" (Hymn 403), the Word of God, and Holy Scriptures (writings).

Suggestions for further reading

The Book of Common Prayer: Collect and Epistle for the Second Sunday in Advent, pages 92–93.

Other articles: Book of Common Prayer, Covenant, Gospel, Revelation, Word of God.

A BISHOP
is a chief pastor in the Church

A BISHOP CONFIRMED YOU or will confirm you. The word *bishop* means "overseer." As the overseer of the clergy and people of his diocese, a bishop is the guardian of the faith, worship, and life of the Church. He represents all that the Church has been, is now, and is to be. That is why in the Episcopal Church *only* a bishop can confirm people. Only bishops can ordain a man, making a layman a deacon or a deacon a priest.

A bishop is the chief shepherd and the spiritual father of all his people, with power and authority to carry on the apostles' teaching and to continue the fellowship of the Church. Through him the Church passes on to its members certain special gifts which Christ has bestowed on it.

A bishop is the head of a diocese. In some dioceses there are also assistant bishops. An assistant is either a bishop coadjutor (who automatically becomes the head of the diocese when the bishop retires or dies) or a bishop suffragan (who remains an assistant). The head of a missionary district is a missionary bishop. He is chosen by the House of Bishops. Some missionary bishops serve in foreign countries.

Suggestions for further reading

The Book of Common Prayer: The service for the Consecrating of Bishops, pages 549–559.

Questions

What can you find out about some bishop's life and work?

THE BOOK OF COMMON PRAYER
*is the Church's authorized handbook
for use when we worship together*

THE BOOK OF COMMON PRAYER is often referred to as the Prayer Book. It is for people to have in their hands so that they may share fully in the worship of God in church. One of the main ideas of our kind of Church is that the people who make up the congregation shall do the worshiping, led by the minister and helped by a prayer book. There are parts that only the minister or priest may say, and parts that it is the people's responsibility to say. If everyone is intended to share in such worship, all must hear or say the same words at the same time. The word *Common* in the title, The Book of Common Prayer, means that all, clergy and laity alike, share the same prayer book. We have it in common.

For this purpose, the Prayer Books we use in church are all uniformly paged. For example, the Venite is on page 9 in all copies; on page 76 are the responses we make when the priest says, "Lift up your hearts." About three-fourths of the Prayer Book consists of selections from the Bible arranged for use in public worship. In certain details, the Prayer Book is printed like the Bible. For instance, though it is full of quotations, it uses no quotation marks, and it never uses a capital letter for a word like *he* or *his* when referring to God. The Psalms and some other parts of the Prayer Book use translations of the Bible older than those most familiar to us.

The Prayer Book includes the services which in earlier days were only to be had in seven separate books. The first Prayer Book services were put into English over four hundred years ago. Since then, they have been translated into at least 150 languages and dialects.

Although the Book of Common Prayer is intended for use in church, you will find many things in it you can use at home. Many families use it together in family prayers.

Questions

What are some of the sacraments, rites, and ceremonies of the Church mentioned on the title page of the Prayer Book? What is the difference between *the Church* and the *Protestant Episcopal Church* as those terms appear on the title page? In how many of the services listed in the table of contents have you taken part?

BURIAL OF THE DEAD
*is the service by which the Church observes
the great event we call death*

IN THE ORDER FOR THE BURIAL OF THE DEAD we show our respect for the body through which we knew the person who has died, and we affirm our faith in his resurrection in

Christ. "I am the resurrection and the life, saith the Lord: he that believeth in me, though he were dead, yet shall he live: and whosoever liveth and believeth in me, shall never die." These words, from the Gospel According to St. John (11:25–26), are the first the priest says, and they give the meaning to the entire service. Because we believe that God raised Jesus from death, we believe that He will raise each one of us who accepts Him as Lord. This faith, this trust, gives us a deep and solemn joy which supports us even in our sadness. "God is our hope and strength, a very present help in trouble." (Prayer Book, page 327)

There are three parts to this service. First, there is a Bible-reading part like Morning or Evening Prayer, with sentences, psalms, and a lesson, followed by prayers. Second, a short service at the grave, where the actual burial takes place. This is the Committal, when we commit the body to the ground "in sure and certain hope of the Resurrection unto eternal life." Third, a collect, epistle, and gospel are provided (pages 268–269) for those who desire to have a special celebration of the Holy Communion.

The Church wants to surround with affection and understanding any member of the fellowship who is separated from someone he loves by death. One of the most important ways we do this is by going to church together for the funeral.

Suggestions for further reading

The Hymnal: 223, 225, 600.
Other articles: Communion of Saints, Death, Easter, Resurrection.

C

CALVARY

*is the name of the hill just outside Jerusalem
where Jesus was crucified*

THE NAME CALVARY occurs only once in the Bible. (Luke
23:33, King James Version). The other name for this hill,
Golgotha, appears three times (Matt. 27:33; Mark 15:22;
John 19:17). By our Lord's death on the Cross we have
been given "new life" that makes it possible for us to live
joyfully and usefully. So the name Calvary has a sacred
meaning for Christians. We find it in many of our hymns:
for example, Hymn 330. Poets have used it often, not
simply to identify the hill but as a word that stands for the
mysterious thing which God accomplished in Christ
through His death.

Suggestions for further reading

Other articles: Atonement, Cross, Death, Passion.

A CANTICLE
*is a short song or songlike composition
used in public worship*

THE WORD *canticle* is related to the word *chant*, and a canticle is usually chanted or sung. The most familiar canticles are found in Morning and Evening Prayer. Those for the Order of the Daily Morning Prayer are:

Venite, page 9   Benedicite, pages 11–13
Te Deum, page 10   Benedictus, page 14
Benedictus es, page 11   Jubilate Deo, page 15

For the Order of the Daily Evening Prayer, the canticles are:

Gloria in excelsis, page 25   Bonum est, pages 27–28
Magnificat, page 26   Nunc dimittis, page 28
Cantate Domino, page 27   Deus misereatur, page 28
              Benedic, anima mea, page 29

There are special canticles to take the place of the Venite at Easter and on Thanksgiving Day.

Most of the canticles are taken directly from the Bible. We still use Latin words as titles for the canticles and psalms because for centuries they were sung in Latin and people got used to thinking of them that way.

Questions

Find out how your minister chooses the canticles for the services. Which are more fitting for one time of year than for another? Do you know the Biblical stories of the Benedictus, the Magnificat, and the Nunc dimittis?

CATHOLIC
means universal, concerning the whole

IT WOULD TAKE A BOOK to explain all the different things the word *Catholic* means. Here are a few of the meanings:

1. *Catholic* refers to the ancient undivided Church. Thus to be a Catholic means to teach all the truth that our Lord taught when He walked with His twelve apostles and told them about God, about Himself, about the Holy Spirit, and about the Church. In this sense the word is used very much as a person might say he is descended "straight from" some famous hero or from someone who came to America on the *Mayflower*.

2. *Catholic* is often used too narrowly in reference to the Roman Catholic Church, whose earthly head is the Bishop of Rome, called the Pope. The members of that branch of the Church are taught that only they are really Catholics.

3. Here is the way Episcopalians use the word: *Catholic* has to do with *wholeness* and *truth*. It means that we honestly try to hold *all* the truth our Lord has taught us, not just our favorite parts. We are not so silly as to think we "know it all." God's truth is much too big. But with the Holy Spirit's help we do our best to hold all that He teaches us through the Bible, through the work of Christian scholars, and through the history of the Church. The Protestant Episcopal Church is Catholic because it teaches and stands up for the Faith for all time, in all countries, and for all people.

The true Church, which faithfully expresses the mind of Christ, is not something you or I thought up. Instead, it is given by God, made by Him, kept going by Him. Reverently we try to find out what He wants His Church to become. In our Creeds we call it the Catholic Church because it strives for wholeness and truth.

Suggestions for further reading

Other articles: Church, Creed, Mission, Pentecost, Protestant.

CHRIST OR MESSIAH
means anointed

THE WORD *Christ* is a title which has become a part of Jesus' name. In ancient times kings were anointed, not crowned; sacred oil was poured over them as a sign of consecration to their office. *Christos* is Greek for *anointed*. The Hebrew word for this is *messiah*. A christ or a messiah, therefore, is one who has been selected for a very important task, such as being a savior or ruler.

The Jewish people felt they needed divine help because man's problems were more than they could handle. They thought the Christ would be (1) a warrior king descended from David, who would first restore the ancient Hebrew kingdom of Israel and then build a world-wide Jewish empire in which God's Law would be obeyed; or (2) a new Moses, who would restate the Law in such a way that everybody would obey it; or (3) a supernatural being who would come to start a whole new period of history.

Jesus *was* the Christ who inaugurated a kingdom, gave the true meaning of the Law, and started a new period in history, but not in the way the Jews expected. He was "the Christ, the Son of the living God"! (Matt. 16:16)

Suggestions for further reading

The Hymnal: 352.

Other articles: Atonement, God, Incarnation, Kingdom of God, Redemption, Trinity.

Questions

In what specific ways would you say Jesus Christ was like the expected Messiah? In what ways was He different? Try to find Old Testament descriptions of the Messiah which accurately fit Jesus Christ.

A CHRISTIAN
is one who believes in Christ and tries to follow Him

CHRIST HAS MADE A TREMENDOUS CHANGE in human history and has won the loyalty of millions of people all over the world. The word *Christian* includes a number of different ideas.

I am a Christian: that is, "I try to let my life be guided and governed by Christian standards. The rules and regulations of society show clearly the influence of Jesus, who taught kindness, courage, and prayer. The true and noble ideal is summed up in the Golden Rule. I believe that the churches are doing a good work. I will support them. I hope that civilization will become more and more Christian as time goes on." Is this all there is to being a Christian?

I am a Christian: that is, I am Christ's man. When I am confirmed I will answer "I do" when the bishop asks, "Do ye promise to follow Jesus Christ as your Lord and Saviour?" The rules of knighthood suggest an example of what this means. In the Middle Ages, when a young man was made a knight, he promised loyalty to his lord. He would serve him, fight for him, even die for him. He promised to "Honour all men. Love the brotherhood. Fear God. Honour the king." (I Pet. 2:17, King James Version) This kind of loyalty means doing not only what we want to do, but even what we may not want, or what we find difficult to do. But is even this all there is to it?

I am a Christian: by baptism I was made "a member of Christ, the child of God, and an inheritor of the kingdom of heaven." This is the way the Book of Common Prayer describes it. (Pages 283 and 577) As a member of Christ I am brother to all other Christians, regardless of color, education, or nationality. St. Paul said, "There is neither Jew nor Greek, there is neither slave nor free, there is neither male nor female; for you are all one in Christ Jesus." (Gal. 3:28) We are Christians not because we are good, but because God in Christ accepts us and forgives us even though we make mistakes and do wrong things. It is God who makes us Christians and strengthens us to help one another.

Suggestions for further reading

The Hymnal: 563.

Other articles: Baptism, Church, Forgiveness, Sacrament, Sin.

CHRISTMAS DAY
*is the feast on which we celebrate the birth
of our Lord Jesus Christ*

DECEMBER 25 IS DESCRIBED in the Book of Common Prayer as "The Nativity of our Lord, or the Birthday of Christ, commonly called Christmas Day." (Page 96) The term

Christmas comes from the old English word *christmasse,* Christ's Mass. Christmastide is the name for the Christmas season which runs to January 6—the famous twelve days of Christmas of the familiar carol.

In very early Christian times believers did not lay as great a stress on our Lord's birthday as on the fact that God's Son had died for us and risen again. Thus they celebrated Easter as commemorating the Resurrection, but it was nearly three hundred years before the Western Church (centering at Rome) set December 25 as the day for the Nativity observance. The Eastern Church (centering at Constantinople) holds a similar observance on January 6. In the West we observe both of these celebrations, making December 25 the time to give thanks for our Lord's incarnation and January 6 the time to celebrate the wonderful ways He was revealed to men as God's Son.

Suggestions for further reading

The Hymnal: 26, 29, 197, 322.
Other articles: Epiphany, Incarnation.

THE CHURCH
*is the Body of which Jesus Christ is the Head
and all baptized people are the members*

WE GO TO CHURCH, a *building,* in which there are services of worship and meetings of many kinds. Here people gather for worship, fellowship, instruction, missionary activities, and the care of those who need help.

The Church is also the *people* who are its members. It is a congregation. Through baptism, we belong to the "congregation of Christ's flock" along with the minister of our parish, the boys and girls in the church school, and adults. But the fellowship of Church people spreads over the whole world. And there's much more to it even than that. We get a glimpse of this larger picture in the Te Deum:

> We praise thee, O God; we acknowledge thee to be the Lord.
> All the earth doth worship thee, the Father ever-lasting.
> To thee all Angels cry aloud; the Heavens, and all the Powers therein;
> To thee Cherubim and Seraphim continually do cry,
> Holy, Holy, Holy, Lord God of Sabaoth;
> Heaven and earth are full of the Majesty of thy glory.
> The glorious company of the Apostles praise thee.
> The goodly fellowship of the Prophets praise thee.
> The noble army of Martyrs praise thee.
> The holy Church throughout all the world doth acknowledge thee . . .

Another glimpse of the extent of the Church is found in the service of Holy Communion: "Therefore with Angels and Archangels, and with all the company of heaven . . ."

The Church is much more than a great family. It is a living Body—the Body of Christ. As you turn your body this way and that, so Jesus guides His Body, the Church. He guides it from inside by the Holy Spirit working in our minds, and He promises that because of the Holy

Spirit's guidance, the *Church as a whole* will never go wrong. So you and I can trust the Church.

The word *church* means an assembly or fellowship. The Jews in Old Testament times were chosen by God to serve Him in the world. Jesus did not found the Church, but re-established the old Jewish fellowship with Himself as Head. After Jesus Christ had risen from the dead, He sent the Holy Spirit to strengthen His followers and bind them together. This fellowship is what we now call Christ's Holy Catholic Church. Its members meet these requirements:

1. They acknowledge that Jesus is their Lord and Saviour.

2. They have been baptized into Him and have received forgiveness of sins.

3. They have received the Holy Spirit.

4. They accept the faith of the Church as contained in the Creeds and hope to grow in their understanding of it.

The Church was not thought up and started by men as an idea of their own. God began it, and God uses the Church to bring us into close fellowship with Him.

The Creeds say that the Church is *one, holy, Catholic,* and *Apostolic.* These four words are also used in the Offices of Instruction, page 291.

1. The Church is one "because it is one Body under one Head." Although Christians are divided, they acknowledge Jesus Christ as Lord and Saviour, and they believe that they should be one. In spite of our disagreements, we are still one family.

2. The Church is holy, not because its members are good, but because the Holy Spirit is at work in the fellowship.

34

3. The Church is Catholic "because it is universal, holding earnestly the Faith for all time, in all countries, and for all people."

4. The Church is Apostolic because it has a commission to go into all the world and because it continues the teaching and fellowship of the apostles. It is sent to preach the Gospel.

The New Testament describes the Church in this way: "But you are a chosen race, a royal priesthood, a holy nation, God's own people, that you may declare the wonderful deeds of him who called you out of darkness into his marvelous light. Once you were no people but now you are God's people; once you had not received mercy but now you have received mercy." (I Pet. 2:9–10)

Suggestions for further reading

The Hymnal: 387, 396, 398.

Other articles: Apostle, Baptism, Catholic, Covenant, Holy Spirit, Mission, Pentecost.

Questions

What is my duty as a member of the Church? (See the Book of Common Prayer, page 291.) What does it mean to call Christians "a chosen race" and "a holy nation"?

THE CHURCH YEAR
is the pattern for the Christian's observance of the great events on which our faith is based

THE CHURCH YEAR begins on the fourth Sunday before Christmas. It is divided into seasons and days. The major seasons are: Advent, Christmastide, Epiphany, Lent, Easter-tide, Ascentiontide, Whitsuntide or Pentecost, and Trinity. Hymn 235 tells briefly what each season celebrates.

A number of Holy Days have to do principally with our Lord and His apostles. A calendar in the front of the Book of Common Prayer shows what these days are and when they occur.

The Christian Year is a calendar whereby we review and relive the main events and beliefs of our faith every year. In doing this, we hear the greatest passages of the Bible. In the course of each year we also hear the whole Gospel.

Each week we observe a little church year. On Friday we recall the passion of our Lord, and Sunday, the first day of the week, is a remembrance of the first Easter.

Suggestions for further reading

Other articles: Advent, Ascension, Easter, Ember Days, Epiphany, Good Friday, Lent, Passion, Pentecost, Roga-tion Days.

CIRCUMCISION
is the Jewish name-giving ceremony

CUTTING, SCARRING, OR TATTOOING some part of the body as a sign of "belonging" has been a custom among primitive peoples. The word *circumcision* comes from the Latin word for cutting.

Among the Jews circumcision was the rite in which a small portion of loose skin was cut from the penis of the male. It came to be thought of as a religious requirement, a seal of the covenant God had made with Abraham. Since the baby Jesus was a Jewish boy, He was circumcised and received His name when He was eight days old. Christian baptism has a purpose somewhat like circumcision. It is the seal of the new covenant in Christ. In it the child receives his name as an individual in God's family.

The Feast of the Circumcision is January 1, the eighth day after Christmas by the Jewish way of counting.

Suggestions for further reading

Other articles: Baptism.

A COLLECT
is a written prayer in which the words are arranged in a pattern

JUST AS WE CAN DIVIDE POEMS into different types of poetry such as the ballad, the sonnet, and the lyric, so we can distinguish between different types of prayer. One of these is the collect.

Almost all collects are short, only a single sentence. But not every short prayer is a collect, for the main thing that makes a prayer a collect is its pattern. Of these patterns, two are easy to recognize.

The first type of collect has a five-part pattern. The prayer opens by calling upon God in some such phrase as "Blessed Lord." A *who clause* follows, mentioning some particular quality in God's character or some other truth about Him: for example, in the collect on page 92 of the Book of Common Prayer, there is the clause "who hast caused all holy Scriptures to be written for our learning." Then comes the *asking clause*, then the hoped-for *result*, and finally the *ending*. A collect built on this pattern is found in the Book of Common Prayer on page 67.

1. Almighty God,
2. unto whom all hearts are open,
all desires known,
and from whom no secrets are hid;
3. Cleanse the thoughts of our hearts
by the inspiration of thy Holy Spirit,
4. that we may perfectly love thee,
and worthily magnify thy Holy Name;
5. through Christ our Lord.

The second type of collect begins with an imperative verb such as "give" or "send." The clause that starts off with this verb is the *asking clause*, in which we ask God for something that we feel we need very much. After that the collect goes on to say what we think will be the happy *result* if God actually gives us the thing we ask Him for. Finally there is the *ending*, usually something like "through Jesus Christ our Lord," which means, "We ask this in the Spirit of Jesus." Here is an example of a collect made on this pattern, found in the Book of Common Prayer on page 218.

1. Grant, we beseech thee, merciful Lord,
to thy faithful people pardon and peace,
2. that they may be cleansed from all their sins,
and serve thee with a quiet mind;
3. through Jesus Christ our Lord.

If you read this out loud you will notice that it is almost poetry. The finest collects have rhythm and balance something like poetry.

38

As you turn the pages of the Book of Common Prayer you will find that most of its collects are written according to one of the two patterns described above, although you may find it interesting to look for other ways in which the collects are composed. You will find that there is a collect for every Sunday and Holy Day.

Suggestions for further reading

Other articles: Prayer, Worship.

Questions

What is your favorite collect? Find one you do not understand.

COMMUNION OF SAINTS
*means the dependence of all of us in the Church
on each other*

IF YOU PLANNED to climb a high mountain, up precipices and over snow and ice, you would go with a party, and the guide would rope you all together so if one slipped the others could hold him or pull him back to safety.

Christians need each other, too. On the long climb to heaven there are many slippery places. We'd be fools to climb alone. We let our Lord "rope" us together in the fellowship of His Church by baptism and confirmation. We draw the rope of fellowship tighter when we receive Holy Communion. If we slip and fall, we let our line of climbers pull us back by absolution.

Who gives us the strongest pull? Why, of course, those who have climbed on ahead—in other words, the saints in heaven. Whether we ask them to or not, whether we even think of them or not, they are "pulling for us" all the time. So it is that our dependence on each other has come to be called *the Communion of Saints*.

Yes, you too are a "saint" in that "Communion." If you were to be careless and take chances, you might pull others down. But even that can be forgiven. When forgiven and back in the Fellowship, you help pull other climbers up to God.

Suggestions for further reading

The Hymnal: 130, 600.
Other articles: Baptism, Saint.

CONFESSION
means owning up to guilt

WHEN A FRIEND OF YOURS admits he has done something wrong, you like and respect him more than ever. He acted like a man; now you know for sure that you can trust him. You do not have to follow his example; nobody would force you to confess. But if you have something on your conscience, you will feel a lot better if you tell it.

There are several ways to own up to something. You may kneel down in your own room at home and tell what's on your mind secretly to God. This is good. You may have a particular sin in mind when you say the General Confession along with everybody else in church. This is good. If you want to, you may tell your fault also to your mother or your father, or anybody else you love and trust. This too is good, because parents who understand are one of

God's best gifts. Finally, you may ask any priest of the church to "hear your confession," that is, to listen while you tell your sins to God and, when you finish, to give you absolution and remission in God's name.

If you confess sincerely, you will know you are forgiven.

Suggestions for further reading

Other articles: Absolution, Forgiveness, Penitence.

CONFIRMATION
is the Laying on of Hands by means of which we receive the strengthening gifts of the Holy Spirit

I AM ALREADY A MEMBER of the Church through being baptized. I am already an American citizen if I was born in this country. But when I am old enough, and understand enough, I need to claim citizenship for myself. When a United States citizen is twenty-one, he can vote; but first he has to register, and he ought to study the issues and what the candidates stand for so that he can vote intelligently. When he is twenty-one, he can also own property in his own name—a piece of land, a house, or a car. He can also be sued. He is responsible.

In confirmation I am received into responsible membership in the life of the Church. The bishop places his hands upon my head and asks God to strengthen me for the job which is mine as a full member of the Church. The service might be compared to the non-Christian ceremonies of American Indians in which a boy becomes a full-fledged brave. He is no longer considered a child; he has become a warrior.

The word *confirm* is used in two ways. First it means to ratify or say "yes" to what someone else has said for us. We *confirm* the promises made for us in baptism. Secondly, it means "to strengthen" as in the Holy Communion where the priest says, "Almighty God . . . confirm and strengthen you in all goodness." (Page 76) We are confirmed and strengthened by the Holy Spirit through this service.

There are two parts to the Order of Confirmation. In the first, the person to be confirmed is presented to the bishop, who represents the whole Church. The candidate hears the lesson, which tells how the early Christian Church used this same ceremony that has come down to us through the ages. (Page 296) If he has a good imagination, the candidate can see more than sixty bishops, one behind another, each with his hands on the head of the man in front of him. The apostles described in the lesson form the beginning of this line; at the end of the line is his own bishop. Here is seen the long life of the Church of which he is a part. He promises the bishop (and so he promises the whole Church) that he will try to live up to the promises made for him when he was baptized. He is now going to stand on his own feet! He *confirms*, or says *"yes"* to, those baptismal promises. In this first part of the service the person being confirmed is the main actor.

In the second part, God the Holy Spirit is the main actor. He *confirms*—that is, strengthens—the person. The bishop lays his hands on the person's head. This action is the "means whereby we receive this grace, and a pledge to assure us thereof." (See "Sacrament.") Thus we follow the ancient practice of the Church. The closing prayers and blessing in this service are not only for the newly confirmed, but for all the people present that they may live according to God's laws.

As baptism makes me a member of the Church, so confirmation strengthens me in this fellowship and helps me fulfill my new responsibilities as a lay person.

Just as the new priest is ordained to his order of ministry in the Church, so by confirmation I am commissioned to the lay order, and have my part to play in the worship and work of the Church.

Suggestions for further reading

The Hymnal: 188.
Other articles: Baptism, Bishop, Faith, Holy Communion.

Questions

Why are most people confirmed at about your age? What things that were promised for us in baptism are we confirming? George Washington was an Episcopal vestryman. Why wasn't he confirmed? What are some of the responsibilities of a lay person?

MY CONSCIENCE
is my understanding of what is right and wrong for me to do and my sense of obligation to do right

MY CONSCIENCE DOES two things for me. It helps me to understand the difference between right and wrong for me, and it demands that I do what I know is right.

But my conscience can sometimes be mistaken, so it is part of my duty to seek for light on all problems of right

43

and wrong and to educate my conscience so that it may guide me properly. It is not enough just to "let my conscience be my guide." I must also see to it that my conscience is guided by the wisdom which comes from God through the things I learn in the Church and through people I love and respect. Every one of us should try to have an intelligent and educated conscience which works in line with God's purpose for us.

We seek to bring our sense of right and wrong in line with God's will. He made us, and He wants us to carry forward His purpose. To keep closely in touch with Him and His purpose is the most important thing in life. Jesus did just this. And He has not left us without help. We have the Bible and the experience of Church members through the centuries. We have prayer, in which we can ask God for His guidance. We have the Holy Communion, through which we are helped to understand what God wants us to do and through which we receive the courage to do it.

God gave us freedom to choose either right or wrong. This freedom is a dangerous gift because it gives us the chance to choose the wrong even when we know it is wrong. So the feeling that we should do right is an important part of living. It is that in us which says, "I ought." If we never said those words to ourselves, we would not be human. We would be only animals. When "I ought" pulls me in one direction and "I want" pulls me in the opposite direction, I have a battle inside myself.

This is the human struggle. Even Jesus had it. He, too, was tempted, but we cannot imagine His wanting to go against His Father. At the very time the battle is going on, our love of what is right can, with God's help, give us victory as it gave Jesus victory. God will help us. He is faithful; that is, He will give us as much power and help as we need for our particular battles, if we ask Him.

If we don't care which way is the right way or if we decide to go against what we know is right, we are in a dangerous situation, for our conscience has gone to sleep.

Suggestions for further reading

The Hymnal: 519, 522.

Other articles: Discipline, Good, Judgment, Law, Right, Sin, Temptation.

Questions

Give some examples of an individual's or a people's conscience being mistaken. What guides us in the growth of conscience?

CONTRITION
see Penitence

A COVENANT
is a solemn agreement

WHEN TOM SAWYER AND HUCKLEBERRY FINN saw Indian Joe in the cave, they entered into a solemn agreement not to tell what they had seen, and they sealed it by pricking their fingers and making a pact in blood. They felt bound by this agreement to be faithful to each other and to keep the promise they had made. When two people or a group of people make a solemn agreement to do something, that is a covenant. They are bound by it and it makes a difference to their whole lives.

The Old Testament says God made a covenant with His people. He promised to be with us, to support us, to strengthen us, to encourage us. We are bound to keep His law and to try to set the kind of example which will encourage other people to live in His way.

The New Testament makes this even stronger through the relationship we have with God in Jesus Christ. His love for us, shown by His suffering and death, requires more of us than any command ever could.

The Bible is the account of the two covenants between God and man. The word *testament* means "covenant." The Old Testament is about the Old Covenant (before Christ) between God and His people, just as the New Testament is about the New Covenant established between God and His people.

The covenant began when Yahweh (the Hebrew name for God) led Abraham to the Promised Land. The descendants of Abraham, whom we call the Jews, continued in this covenant. Moses, the great prophet-leader of Israel, heard God telling him, "I am your God; you are my people." He built an altar for the worship of God and took the blood of animals and dashed part of it on the altar and part of it on the people. The meat of the animals he also divided between God and the people by burning some on the altar and giving the rest to the people to eat. In this sacramental way God and the people shared one food and "became one body." It was a covenant, and it was "sealed" —made sure—in something shared. The Hebrews became a people bound to God. This story is told in Exodus, Chapters 19 through 20.

As time passed, God revealed to His prophets that He loved *all men*. Christians believe that God sent Jesus Christ to make a new covenant with all men. It was a new relationship, made in love, between God and all mankind.

We are sharers in this covenant. As the Old Covenant was sealed by a holy meal, so the New Covenant is sealed by a holy meal, the Holy Communion. "This is my blood of the new covenant [testament]," said our Lord. We make this joyful truth clear and plain in the breaking of the bread and the pouring of the wine in a Family Covenant Meal. The Holy Communion constantly renews the oneness of God's people with their Lord and with one another.

Suggestions for further reading

The Hymnal: 239, 298.
Other articles: Church, Cross, Holy Communion, Law.

TO COVET
is to desire wrongfully what belongs to someone else

IT IS NOT WRONG to want things. But it is very wrong to want something that belongs to someone else so keenly that you will scheme to get it or will hurt the person who has it. It is not wrong to want a dress like a school friend's or a ball glove like another fellow's. It is normal to be ambitious for honors. But when this natural urge injures a relationship with others, it becomes covetousness.

Sally was elected May Queen by a few votes over Jane. Jane had set her heart on being May Queen. She felt very bitter about the election and found herself daydreaming that she was the one who had been chosen. Her daydreams turned into envy of Sally, and she began to spread false rumors. She said she knew someone who had seen Sally vote for herself seven times, so there ought to be another election. This was certainly mean. And what had caused it? Covetousness.

Rivalry is fine if one person does not hurt another, or cheat another, or do his work in a mean and unfriendly way. We can see why one of the Commandments is: "Thou shalt not covet." As soon as we begin to covet a thing that belongs to someone else, the friendly feeling of brotherliness and of belonging together disappears. Covetousness can lead to many other sins against our neighbors. This is true everywhere—at home, in athletics, at school, in business. The covetousness of nations for raw materials and natural resources can lead even to war.

Suggestions for further reading

Other articles: Conscience, Good, Law, Murder, Sin, Temptation.

Questions

If your friend gets an English bike and you want one, too, is that covetousness? If not, can it become covetousness? If you are covetous, how can you get over it?

CREATION
is God's act of making everything

To SAY THAT GOD is the Creator of all things means that we did not make the world or ourselves. Behind the whole process of being made or born, God's creative love was at work.

We know something of what creation is like because we

make things ourselves. When we go to a workbench or to a sewing machine or typewriter, we carry out an idea that we have. We have a purpose in mind, whether it is to make a birdhouse, a dress, a story, a picture, or a landscape. What we turn out may not be perfect, but we keep on.

Whatever we make has to be shaped out of something else God has made. But *God* created everything out of nothing! The Bible tells us this. It doesn't tell us how He did it. Science is beginning to discover some of the ways, but the Bible tells us that *God did it.*

You can read stories of the Creation in the Bible in Genesis 1:1—3:24. God created everything and keeps on creating. God made persons. He does not treat us as puppets on the end of a string. Like Adam and Eve, we can rebel against Him and feel lonely. Like Cain, we can have murderous feelings. When God made us, He gave us freedom. That is why we can hurt each other in all sorts of ways.

On the other hand, part of God's purpose is to create persons who are able to love Him as He loves us. Even God cannot buy love. But he made us so that we are free to love Him, and He keeps helping us to love Him and our fellows. God continues to be the Creator and to keep His universe in existence, for the world is incomplete and keeps developing according to His purpose.

Suggestions for further reading

The Hymnal: 548.
Other articles: Almighty, Faith, God, Love.

Questions

Why do you think God created the universe? How do

our wrong acts hinder God's plan? Why don't our wrong acts stop God's plan?

A CREED
is an official statement of important things believed

WHEN WE STAND UP TOGETHER and say the Creed out loud, we speak with one voice. We declare our trust in the same God who has been loved and trusted through the many centuries of our Christian faith. It is like saying, "This is the God we believe in!" Saying it that way, all together, gives us a sense of belonging. It helps us to renew our faith, to remind ourselves how much we trust in God and how much we need Him. It pledges our allegiance to God.

When we say the Creed, we are not merely saying that we share an opinion with other people, but we are identifying ourselves with the fellowship which lives by this faith. We are saying, I belong to the age-old, world-wide fellowship of Christian people. This faith has been held by millions of people before me; it is also held by millions of people living in the world today; and it will be held by generations that come after me.

The Creed does not talk about how we feel. It talks about what God is—our loving heavenly Father. It tells us what God did and does as our Saviour and Friend. It tells us what He did and does for us through the Holy Spirit. It tells us what He will do in judging us and in bringing us to live with Him forever.

Our Book of Common Prayer has two creeds, the Apostles' Creed and the Nicene Creed. These Creeds, which belong to the Christian Church everywhere, were written long ago. The origins of the Apostles' Creed can be traced back to the end of the second century. The Nicene Creed got its name from the council of the Church at Nicaea in A.D. 325. But it did not reach its present form until several centuries later.

Some of the old words, such as *quick*, have changed their meaning. If we were to write these Creeds for the first time today, we would undoubtedly use the word *living* rather than quick. When we say "Amen" after the Creed, we are saying, "I believe what this Creed proclaims." The fact that our Church cares about the meaning of the Creeds, and not just about the words, is seen in the little note printed in the middle of page 15 of the Book of Common Prayer.

Suggestions for further reading

Other articles: Almighty, Amen, Ascension, Atonement, Belief, Catholic, Church, God, Holy Spirit, Incarnation, Resurrection, Saint, Second Coming, Sin, Trinity.

Questions

Why isn't it enough to say, "I believe in Christ"?

THE CROSS
is the most sacred of all Christian symbols

IF YOU HAD LIVED in Jesus' time and were a highway robber, or had threatened a revolution, or had encouraged a crowd to get out of control, you probably would have been crucified.

Those who schemed to get rid of Jesus could have had

Him murdered quietly. However, they wanted to have Him executed in public, with all the suffering and shame of crucifixion. Remember that Jesus freely accepted this death "for us men and for our salvation."

That is why the Cross is the symbol both of Jesus' death and of His resurrection. He who died on a cross rose victorious over death. By His death and resurrection He brought us all back to God. So the Cross stands on our altars as a sign of victory. It is the sign of a new covenant between God and man.

And you, as a member of the Church, are in this new relationship with God. By Christ's power you can turn your misfortunes and suffering into victory. When you do this, you have a part in Christ's work.

Suggestions for further reading

The Hymnal: 336, 337.

Other articles: Atonement, Calvary, Mediator, Reconciliation, Redemption, Resurrection, Saviour, Symbol.

Questions

When a person has a serious illness, why is it sometimes referred to as a "cross he has to bear"? Why do the Jews use the Tables of the Law as a symbol?

D

A DEACON
*is a minister who assists a priest in church
services and in parish work*

WHEN A LAYMAN IS FIRST made a minister, he is ordained
deacon. This ordination gives him the duty of working
with a priest under the direction of a bishop. His special
work is to take care of those in need and to assist at the
Holy Communion. These duties are described in the service for his ordination and on page 294 in the Book of
Common Prayer. He may not preach without the permission of his bishop; he may not celebrate the Holy Communion or pronounce the Absolution or the Blessing. He
may not be the rector of a parish but may be in charge of
a mission.

His training normally includes four years of college and
three years in seminary. Then he has to take examinations
in Church history, the Bible, theology, preaching, Christian
education, and other subjects.

In most cases, a deacon, after about a year, is advanced
to the priesthood. In other words, after he has proved himself acceptable and has passed additional examinations, he

is advanced to the next higher order of the ministry. Occasionally, in special circumstances, a man chooses to remain a deacon permanently.

The word *deacon* means "servant" or "minister," and this is the title Jesus chose for Himself. He said also, "Whoever would be great among you must be your servant [deacon]." (Matt. 20:26) So the office of deacon represents in a wonderful way the meaning of Christian ministry.

Suggestions for further reading

Other articles: Bishop, Layman, Minister, Priest.

Questions

Can you tell whether a minister is a deacon or a priest by looking at him? If you were a rector of a church, what jobs would you give a deacon to do?

THE DEATH
of the body occurs when physical life leaves it

THE OLD TESTAMENT recognizes the fact that we all die. But the death of Jesus Christ brought an enormous change in the way people thought about death. The New Testament teaches us that Christ Himself experienced death and in so doing destroyed its power. He rose from the dead. The resurrection of Christ and our resurrection through Him are the great, new facts. A Christian does not have to be afraid of death, but he must still prepare to meet God, who will see him as he is.

When a person dies, especially someone you love, you

naturally have great sorrow. The Church understands this and does not pretend that it is not so. But it helps you overcome your sorrow by holding up a mighty truth that is even stronger than death. When you go to a funeral in church, the very first words you hear in the service are: "I am the resurrection and the life, saith the Lord: he that believeth in me, though he were dead, yet shall he live: and whosoever liveth and believeth in me, shall never die."

In this service you learn that those whom you have known and loved are still united with you in God's love. The dead are alive in Him, because God keeps all things in His care.

What you believe about God and about Jesus Christ makes all the difference to you. Not only life but even death takes on a new meaning, for even in death you are not cut off from God. He made you and will uphold you in this life and in the life to come. (See St. John 14:1–2.) The prayer on pages 74–75 of the Book of Common Prayer speaks of our "continual growth" in His love. We are to serve Him now and hereafter, not as ghosts but, like our Lord, as complete persons.

Suggestions for further reading

The Hymnal: 91, 223.

Other articles: Burial of the Dead, Calvary, Easter, Heaven, Hell, Judgment, Resurrection, Saint, Soul and Spirit.

Questions

In the Order for the Burial of the Dead, why do you think there is no place to recount the deeds of the person who has died? Why do we pray for the dead? Why do we pray for ourselves?

DEPENDENCE
is leaning upon someone for help

FROM THE VERY BEGINNING of our lives, we need someone to love us and care for us. There must be somebody we can depend on for support and understanding, some person who will always stand by us. This leaning on someone who can help us do things we cannot do alone is called dependence.

Naturally we depend at first on our parents for food, warmth, care, and, above all, for love. When we are older, we may also depend on a teacher, friends, a husband or wife. But our dependence upon these people is not complete. They will not be with us forever, and, even if they were, they would sometimes fail us without meaning to do so. We want to stand on our own feet much of the time. This helps us grow up. Independence is important, too.

There are degrees of dependence. We depend more on some things than on others. If I see a new bridge and decide to walk on it, I depend upon the steel and concrete, but I depend *still more* on the engineer who designed it. And when I begin to think about it, I see that I am depending most of all on the One who made the engineer!

We need to depend on someone who never fails. That Someone is God. The Bible describes God's dependableness in many ways. "Underneath are the everlasting arms." (Deut. 33:27) "God, the Lord, is my strength." (Hab. 3:19) "God is faithful." (I Cor. 1:9)

The psalmist was thinking of the dependability of God when he wrote:

"I will love thee, O Lord, my strength. The Lord is my stony rock, and my defence;

"My Saviour, my God, and my might, in whom I will trust; my buckler, the horn also of my salvation, and my refuge.

"I will call upon the Lord, which is worthy to be praised; so shall I be safe from mine enemies." (Psalm 18: 1–3, Book of Common Prayer, page 359)

Suggestions for further reading

The Hymnal: 551 (stanzas 1, 2).
Other articles: Faith, God, Love.

Questions

Would you like to be totally independent of your parents right now?

THE DEVIL (SATAN, BEELZEBUB)
is the spiritual enemy of God and man

THERE IS SO MUCH EVIL in the world we naturally think that some powerful being must be in charge of it, like the general of a wicked army. Whatever may be the truth about that, we do know that life is an endless battle. The time never comes when we can say, "Now we can take it easy," and have no trouble being good people ever after.

The Devil represents all the forces seeking to defeat the will of God. This picture of a devil who works against our better selves is vivid and helps make clear to us the struggle between right and wrong.

As angels represent the agencies of God to help us, so demons represent the evil power that enters into us to plague us. This makes it harder for us to be good. Jesus spoke about casting out devils, and He also described someone as being bound by Satan. The demons recognized Jesus as their enemy, and He cast them out in God's Name. (Mark 5:1–20; Matt. 12:22–32) Through the Cross and Resurrection our Lord proved Himself the victor over evil. By His strength we can be victors, too.

Suggestions for further reading

The Book of Common Prayer: page 117.
Other articles: Angels.

Questions

Why are angels drawn as perfect beings and devils as a mixture of man and beast? Why don't people talk about casting out demons today? What does someone mean who says, "The Devil has got into you"?

A DISCIPLE
is one who follows and learns from another person

WE USUALLY THINK OF THE WORD *disciple* as referring to twelve of Jesus' followers. Actually a disciple is anyone who is learning from some other person. If you trust an older person and want to be with him and learn from him, you are his disciple. When you grow older you may study medicine or law or art under a leader in your field. The late Associate Justice of the Supreme Court, Oliver Wendell Holmes, each year used to invite the highest ranking student in the graduating class of the Harvard University Law School to be his clerk. This was regarded as a great honor because the student could be with Justice Holmes and learn from him.

In Palestine in Biblical times a young person often went to a rabbi and became his disciple. He could change his mind, however, and go to another rabbi if he found one whom he trusted more. Jesus' disciples were first of all men whom He invited to join Him, but they didn't have to do so unless they wanted to. Some men turned the invitation down. (See the story of the rich young man in the Gospel According to St. Matthew 19:16-22.) Besides the disciples who were closest to Jesus, the Bible says that there were many more, including women and children.

Every Christian is a disciple of Jesus because he learns from Jesus and tries to follow Him.

Suggestions for further reading

The Hymnal: 575.
Other articles: Apostle, Image, Layman, Mission, Saint.

Questions

Who are some heroes living today whom you would like to follow?

DISCIPLINE
is training which strengthens and corrects

THE WORDS *discipline* and *disciple* look very much alike. We usually think of *discipline*, first, as maintaining order and, second, as punishment. It is more than these.

A *discipline* is a program of learning which helps you

make a branch of knowledge or skill your own. Music lessons and practice are a discipline. If you do not use your fingers properly or get the right time or hit the right notes, the teacher tells you what is wrong. The teacher also plans exercises to be used in practice. The purpose is to play the piano. When a football team begins the season, the coach works over and over again on such things as blocking, tackling, passing, and running. There are right ways to do these things and wrong ways. He wants the players to learn the right ways so thoroughly that in the game they will use them naturally.

Another purpose of discipline is to put a person back on the track so he can get on with the job. The purpose of order in the classroom, for example, is to let the class do its work. There is no point in having a group of people sitting around quietly for the sake of sitting around quietly.

The purpose of punishment is to help those who get out of line get back into line. Real discipline must result in self-discipline if it is to work. We can't always have other people telling us what to do and correcting us when we are wrong. Our teachers try to help us learn skills so that we can use them ourselves when they are called for. A self-disciplined person is able to know when to use a skill and how to use it, without anybody telling him.

Suggestions for further reading

Other articles: Conscience, Disciple, Lent, Obey.

Questions

Does punishment have any place in parental discipline of children? In God's discipline? Have you talked to your rector about a rule of life for your own discipline?

E

EASTER
is the anniversary of the Resurrection

THE MOST IMPORTANT THING ABOUT EASTER is that Jesus Christ rose from the dead. Jesus died and was buried like other people, but He rose from the dead. Because He is the divine Son of God, what happened to Him is of greatest importance to us all.

Read the reports for yourself in the Gospels: St. Matthew 28, St. Mark 16; St. Luke 24; St. John 20–21. There are the facts. Here is what our Church says they mean: (1) that Jesus really died; (2) that He really came to life again in His body as well as in His soul; (3) that His body after His resurrection was in a new condition, able to appear and disappear and to do other things that our bodies at present cannot do; but it was still a real body, just as real as ours.

The Church, therefore, proclaimed that Jesus Christ is the God-Man. (Rom. 1:4) This is what the Nicene Creed means when it says that Jesus, to whom we pray, whom we worship, and whom we serve, is "God of God, Light of Light, Very God of very God" and was made man in order to bring us all into communion with God.

The Gospels tell us that on the night Jesus was arrested, Peter denied he even knew Him. But a few days later in the Temple square, Peter showed that he was a new person. He knew that Jesus was still alive. He knew that the world had things backward and that the only way to put them right was for people to turn to this very same Jesus as Saviour and Lord. For, in spite of all the things men had done to Him, our Lord loved us enough to come right back among us as a man and give us His new life. He gives that new life to us when we are baptized. He continues to give it to us every time we receive Holy Communion. Through His living body He gives us life. When we let Christ overcome our pride and selfishness, we find that we. can become new people with a new point of view and a new courage and a new hope. Thus discovering the meaning of Easter can be the most important discovery anybody can make.

Suggestions for further reading

The Hymnal: 85, 91, 95, 96.

Other articles: Calvary, Cross, Heaven, Hell, Kingdom of God, Resurrection, Soul and Spirit.

Questions

What are Easter pageants intended to do? Why should all of us receive Holy Communion on Easter Day?

EMBER DAYS
are days when we pray for those who are preparing to enter the ministry

THE EMBER DAYS occur four times a year: spring, summer, autumn, winter. They are always Wednesday, Friday, and Saturday in the same week. The springtime Ember Days come right after the First Sunday in Lent; the summertime, right after Whitsunday; those for autumn, after September 14; for winter, after December 13.

At these times the Church invites us to pray for all who are preparing to become ministers. We ask the Holy Spirit to strengthen and guide them both in their studies and in learning more about people.

The laws of our Church require that during his three years in seminary a man shall either write a letter to his bishop or go to see him and have a talk with him some time during every Ember Week.

Suggestions for further reading

The Hymnal: 217, 220.

The Book of Common Prayer: Special prayers for all of us to use on the Ember Days, pages 38, 39, and 260.

Other articles: Bishop, Deacon, Minister, Priest, Vocation.

Questions

What steps would you take if you wanted to become a minister? What work in the Church is open to women?

THE EPIPHANY
*is the feast day when we give thanks that God
made Himself known to all the world in Jesus Christ*

THE DATE OF THIS FESTIVAL is January 6. The Gospel for the Feast of the Epiphany is the story of the wise men who came to visit the infant Christ, bringing Him costly gifts. They are often spoken of as kings, as in the carol "We three kings of Orient are," but it is more likely that they were scholars who studied the stars. The important thing is that they represented the various peoples of the earth, especially non-Jews, called Gentiles.

The Wise Men are often pictured as members of three different races: one white, one Negro, and one Oriental. This suggests that all races need Christ. Sometimes they are pictured as a very old man, a middle-aged man, and a youth, since people of all ages need Him.

Amahl and the Night Visitors, by Gian-Carlo Menotti, is a modern opera about Epiphany. Watch for it on television during the Christmas season.

Suggestions for further reading

The Hymnal: 46, 49, 258, 263.
Other articles: Mission.

Questions

If Jesus were born today, what gifts would you like to give Him? Why do "the Magi," instead of Santa Claus, bring gifts to Mexican children?

AN EPISTLE
in the New Testament is a letter of special importance about the Christian faith

WHENEVER WE WRITE A LETTER to someone, we usually *tell* him about ourselves and what we are doing and *ask* him to do something, even if it is only to tell us about himself.

In the New Testament there are books called Epistles: letters to the early churches from St. Paul and other leaders.

64

St. Paul wrote to congregations in Rome, Corinth, Philippi, and elsewhere to explain things about the Christian faith, to give them advice, and to tell the people what he was doing. The people thought these letters so good that they copied them and shared them with other churches. Eventually, when the New Testament was put together, the letters were thought so practical and useful, so deeply moving and inspiring, that they were put in the Bible.

When a passage from one of the Epistles is read in church, it isn't only advice from the writer to a congregation of the early Church, but advice to us, too. Sometimes in the Holy Communion a selection from the Old Testament or the Book of Acts is used "for the Epistle." We should listen to the Epistles as if they were addressed to us.

Suggestions for further reading

The Hymnal: 403.
Other articles: Bible, Gospel.

Questions

What kind of epistle would St. Paul write to your class? What advice would he give you? What do you think St. Paul meant by calling *us* Epistles? (II Cor. 3:2–3)

F

FAITH
is the response of a person to one he trusts

ONCE A YOUNG GIRL was frightened crossing a narrow plank bridge, but she had faith in her big brother, and he held her hand. She still had to do her own walking, but she had confidence her brother would get her across.

When you learned to swim, you needed to get over your fear that you would sink. As soon as you trusted the water to hold you up, you could swim and even float!

A Christian says: "I must do the best I can with what I have here and now. My confidence is that God cares about me, even though I do not always succeed in what I am asked to do. God loves me, no matter what. That is my faith."

We use the word *faith* in a different way in the expression "the Faith." The Faith refers to things which a Christian "ought to know and believe to his soul's health."

Suggestions for further reading

The Hymnal: 563.
Other articles: Belief, Grace, Justification by Faith.

66

THE FALL

is the word used to describe man's separation from God

GOD CREATED MAN to live with Him always; He intended that man should be in the fullest and happiest kind of fellowship with Him. But the terrible fact is that people are not living that way. Another fact is that their own best efforts simply cannot bring them into that fellowship with their Creator.

The Bible tells us about the Fall in a story in the Book of Genesis. The story is not meant to be taken as literally true history; it is a story which applies to everybody and was written by an ancient Jewish writer who was trying to express, in the form of a legend, the facts which he knew to be true. The story says that at first man lived in a beautiful garden (that is, in complete happiness) and in perfect relations with God. Then, because he chose to disobey a rule which had been made to protect this happiness, he found himself separated from God (exiled from the garden) and unable to get back.

Whatever you may question of the details of the story, it gives the real truth about you and me and every other man who has lived in the world—except Jesus Christ, who was God's perfect Son. All of us, except Christ, are separated from God; all of us, except Christ, have to be brought back to Him. The story says: (1) God made us to be happy with Him; (2) we are separated from Him by sin, not only our own actual sins but the sinfulness of our whole human race; (3) only God can bring us back to Himself. Those three facts are what the Fall is all about. The story is told about you and me.

The Gospel which the Church proclaims tells us that in

Christ, God took action which did bring us back to Him. If we let Christ give us His Spirit, incorporating us into the family of the Church, we are again "at one" with God. Jesus Christ is the perfect Son whom God gave to the world to bring you and me back to the plan which God has for all His children.

Suggestions for further reading

The Hymnal: 58.
Other articles: Atonement, Fellowship, Redemption, Sin.

TO BEAR FALSE WITNESS
is to tell a lie about another person

IF YOU UNTRUTHFULLY BLAME another person for having done something that you yourself did, hoping that he will be punished for it instead of you, you are bearing false witness. It is an attack on the other person's character, an attack on the person himself, and so it becomes a kind of murder or at least a crippling injury.

There are other kinds of false witness. Suppose a group of people are whispering together, and, as you get near them, you hear them talking against somebody you know. Perhaps they are laughing, and their voices show that they feel themselves to be better than the person they are talking about. If you join them and add to the laughter and also to the ideas—if you take part in injuring the person who is being talked about—then you are as guilty as they are. All of you are bearing false witness against a neighbor. Even if some of the mean things being said are true, you are going against the Ninth Commandment in spirit, for you are doing something to hurt your neighbor. You have cast him out as if you had slammed a door in his face. Read the Epistle of St. James, 3:1–12.

This kind of evil gossip has done a lot of harm to many people. Starting a rumor is like starting a fire in the woods during a dry spell. One little spark can begin it, but it may take days of hard labor and the risk of many lives to put it out.

Fists and knives are not the only things that bruise and cut. Words can do the same, and they can hurt where the pain and injury will last a long, long time.

Suggestions for further reading

The Book of Common Prayer: page 289.

Other articles: Conscience, Devil, Law, Murder, Sin, Trespass, Witness.

Questions

What are some examples of the harm that gossip can do? What is perjury?

A FAMILY

is a group of people who belong together because they are related, married, or adopted

YOUR FAMILY IS very important. Whether it is large or small, rich or poor, you are still a part of it. When you feel you are loved, cared for, wanted, forgiven, you are happy about belonging. Even when you are "out of step" and think you hate the other members of your family, you still belong.

Christian families are not the only families in which members feel they belong. But a Christian family is different in the way they worship and respond to God, and let Him influence their lives. The Church emphasizes the importance of families worshiping together.

When the Jews before Christ's time sometimes called God "Father," they were thinking of Him as the one who had made them His own family. As His family, they were required to keep His laws. Jesus accepted all this but added that God really loves His people.

Do you remember the story of the Prodigal Son (Luke 15:11–32)? The father hopes and prays that the boy will come back and live as a member of the family again. The father must have watched for his son every day, because he sees him in the distance, runs to meet him, and hugs him. Before the boy can finish saying what is on his mind, the father interrupts with orders to the servants for his son's comfort and for celebrating his return. Although the older brother was jealous and tried to refuse the younger boy a place in the family, the father's love was big enough for both of them. Jesus was saying that God's generosity and forgiveness are at least as great as this.

The chief way we know that the Father loves us is that He sent His Son, Jesus Christ, who was willing to give Himself and to suffer for others. In Him we see God loving His people.

A Christian family seeks to have that same kind of love. Our Lord said to His disciples, "This is my commandment, that you love one another as I have loved you." (John 15:12)

Suggestions for further reading

The Hymnal: 504.
Other articles: Fellowship, God, Love, Reconciliation.

Questions

In what way is the Church "the family of God"?

FASTING
is going without food

IF YOU GO TO your grandmother's for Thanksgiving and she roasts a fat turkey for you and bakes pies, you will please her if you eat all you can. If you were to eat only a little, as if you didn't like what she had cooked, she would be hurt. You make her happy when you pass your plate for more.

Good food comes from God and He, too, loves to see us enjoy it. We shall enjoy it, He hopes, not like pigs, but like human beings who know enough to thank Him. Part of being thankful is really to enjoy the food. Joy comes from God.

Why, then, did Jesus go without food for "forty days"?[1] It was partly because of what happened when He was baptized. In a flash of clear vision, He saw heaven open and the Holy Spirit came down upon Him like a dove, and He heard the Father say, "Thou art my beloved Son." After that experience, He had to be quiet and think. He went out into the desert where no one would disturb Him, where He could be alone with His Father and pray as long

---

[1] "Forty days" may be just a Jewish way of saying "a long time."

as He liked. He knew there was no food there, but thought that was a fair price to pay.

But Jesus meant more by His fast than that. To Him, fasting was a kind of prayer. It was a way of saying to His Father, "I love You more than anything in the world."

Jesus did not tell us to fast; He *assumed* that we would. *When* we fast, He said, we are not to make a show of it but to do it secretly so that only our Father in heaven will know.

In the introductory part of the Prayer Book, on page li, the Episcopal Church asks us to fast on Ash Wednesday and Good Friday and to use "abstinence" on the forty days of Lent, on the Ember Days, and on most Fridays.

You can see why the Church picks out those days. On Ash Wednesday we recall that Jesus went into the desert to fast and pray for forty days. He did this for us, so we keep those days in fellowship with Him. Ember Days are days of special prayer for those who are to be ordained as ministers. We pray for them not only in words but also by the action of fasting. On Good Friday Jesus gave up His life for us all, and in thanksgiving we give up something not only on that Friday but on almost every Friday in the year.

The Prayer Book does not tell us *what* we are to give up on those days or how much of it. But though our Church lays down no laws on this, it has some very old family customs. A great many Church people, for instance, keep Friday by giving up meat. This is done as an offering to Jesus who died on Friday. Such fasting draws us closer to each other in His family.

Another family custom of ours is not to eat anything just before we receive Holy Communion. This is our way of telling Jesus we love Him more than our food. It helps us feel our need for Him.

Our other fasting customs, the ones that call for real cutting down on food, are intended for adults. If younger Christians want to keep Ember Days and days of Lent, they should deny themselves in some other way. And we should all, old and young, remember *why* we give things up: to help us make "extraordinary acts and exercises of devotion," that is, to pray to God more than we usually would.

Suggestions for further reading

The Hymnal: 55, 59.
Other articles: Good Friday, Lent.

FELLOWSHIP
to the Christian means the family feeling
of those who belong to Christ

ANY GROUP OF PEOPLE who enjoy being together because they care for each other have formed a "fellowship." Even people who live far apart and have never seen each other belong to a fellowship if they work together for some great cause, such as peace or perhaps the wiping out of a disease.

There can also be groups which have not built any fellowship. For example, a work crew hired to do a job may or may not be a fellowship. It depends upon how the members treat one another. If they care about each other's welfare and help each other, fellowship exists among them.

But for Christians, fellowship means much more than that. It means belonging to each other because we all belong to our Lord.

"Join hands, then, brothers of the faith,
Whate'er your race may be!
Who serves my Father as a son
Is surely kin to me.

"In Christ now meet both East and West,
In him meet South and North,
All Christly souls are one in him,
Throughout the whole wide earth."

Christian fellowship is seen at its best when the Church is doing its real job—loving people and bringing them into its family. In this Family, we care for each other because Christ loves us all. The bond of Christian fellowship is so strong that with God's help we can break down the feeling of distrust between races and nations. In the long run, nothing can keep Christians apart because our Lord has made us one Family.

Suggestions for further reading

The Hymnal: 263, 495.
Other articles: Acceptance, Church, Family, Redemption, Rejection.

Questions

How does the fellowship of the Church differ from that experienced in the Hi-Y, the Scouts, the Stamp Club, and so on?

FORGIVENESS

is giving up your claim to whatever a person owes you for having offended or hurt you

IF YOU BREAK A NEIGHBOR'S WINDOW while playing ball, you can pay for it, and your good relationship with your neighbor is maintained. The debt is paid, but there is not necessarily any forgiveness.

Suppose, however, your neighbor says, "I'm going to take down this fence between your yard and mine so you fellows will have a bigger field to play on." How would you feel?

You don't think he would do that? Well, that is what forgiveness is like. It is more than canceling a debt. It is reaching out to the person who did wrong and showing him that he is still a good friend.

If you apologize, or say you are sorry, that is one-sided. But when the other person does something for you, and you know everything is all right between you, then you are forgiven. Forgiving is giving by the person who was hurt or offended. The person who does the wrong can't do any more than *ask* to be forgiven.

Sometimes we don't *say*, "I forgive you," but we show it by action. Two friends had quarreled bitterly. Molly finally cooled down and knew she had said too much, but she still had too much pride to admit it. So she went out and walked past Sue's house. Sue was at the window. When Molly passed the second time, Sue went to the door and said, "Come in and have a Coke." Molly knew she was forgiven. Both girls realized how their friendship had been shaken. They looked at each other over the Coke bottles and suddenly laughed happily. If we try to forgive and really succeed, we may find that we have healed our own hurts, too.

Being forgiven doesn't mean you get out of punishment. A parent may punish you to help you learn what things you should not do, but he still forgives you. Sometimes, through this, you understand him better and know how much he loves you. But if a school authority or a law court has to punish you, you may never feel any love. You haven't been forgiven—you've just "got what was coming to you." God is a loving Father as well as a Judge, and therefore He forgives.

The Lord's Prayer says, "forgive us our trespasses, as we forgive those who trespass against us." Here we are asking God to forgive us. We are also admitting that we should forgive everyone who hurts us since we count on God's forgiveness. It may be very hard to forgive. For a while we may be cross, rebellious, and unforgiving. God still loves us. He is always ready to take us as we are and then *help* us to be sorry, to confess, and to forgive others.

You may hear someone say, "I can forgive, but I can't forget." There is no reason why he should forget. Memory is one part of us, and loving people is another. But if we really forgive a friend or a teacher or even a parent, we take him just as he is. The mistake he made is part of him. We may not forget the mistake, but we don't keep telling ourselves about it over and over. Instead, we tell ourselves, "I like him anyway. I've done things just as bad (or even worse). God always forgives *me*."

Jesus Christ lived as man and died on the Cross so that we might know how God's love reaches down to us, no matter what we do. He not only loves us, but He gives us the courage to ask for and receive forgiveness.

76

Suggestions for further reading

The Hymnal: 345, 499.

Other articles: Absolution, Atonement, Conscience, Grace, Judgment, Redemption, Sin, Trespass.

Questions

How do we find the power to forgive others? What are some of the ways in which you know your parents have forgiven you? Can you find some words in the Prayer Book services that help people realize God forgives them?

G

GOD

GOD CANNOT BE DEFINED. We know He is perfect love, joy, beauty, wisdom, holiness: before Him even angels tremble.

He deserves absolutely and completely to be adored; and He is exciting—more exciting than all adventures.

God does not need any help from outside Himself. He was not made by anyone, but He made all things. He never began. He simply IS. He has been, for ever and ever, and He will be, for ever and ever.

God is personal, but in a far more excellent way than we are personal. He is sheer invisible spirit. For example, He needs no body. It is true that God the Son took a body when He, "for us men and for our salvation . . . was made man." In that body He died for us and rose again and ascended into heaven. But except for Christ's human body, God has no body at all.

Everything—the whole universe—was created by God, and He keeps it going moment by moment. If He did not, everything would vanish.

God never changes. But He causes His creation to change, for He is the ruler of all things. And He knows all things and is everywhere.

Above all, God is love. And His love is so great and so strong that nothing can break it. He loves each one of us, as if each were the only one. He will love us forever.

There is, and can be, only one God. People have sometimes thought differently. They have split up their idea of God into many little "gods" and "goddesses." But God revealed to the Jews that He is One. "Hear, O Israel: The LORD our God is one LORD. . . ." (Deut. 6:4) That saying is taught to every Jewish child. In the past it was painted on the doorposts of the houses and upon the gates. Men wore it in small rolls of parchment on their foreheads and on the left arm near the heart. That God is One is central to the Jewish faith and to our own.

But God's *one*ness is not lonely. He is One; yet in a strange, wonderful way He is also Three—the Father, the Son, and the Holy Ghost.

God is mysterious. The most brilliant human mind will never understand Him completely. That is one reason why heaven will be so wonderful. Always it will be new to us and full of adventure as God unfolds one glorious secret after another about Himself and the myriad things He has created.

Therefore with Angels and Archangels, and with all the company of heaven, we laud and magnify thy glorious Name; evermore praising thee, and saying,

HOLY, HOLY, HOLY, Lord God of hosts, Heaven and earth are full of thy Glory: Glory be to thee, O Lord Most High. Amen.

Suggestions for further reading

The Hymnal: 274, 466, 523.
The Book of Common Prayer: Venite, page 9.
Other articles: Almighty, Atonement, Creation, Grace, Holy Spirit, Incarnation, Judgment, Kingdom of God, Redemption, Saviour, Trinity.

Questions

If there were nothing but God, could He still love? What are some of the many ways in which He has revealed Himself?

GODPARENTS OR SPONSORS
are those who promise at a child's baptism to be responsible for his Christian training

WHEN A BABY IS BAPTIZED, he becomes a member of God's family, the Church. To be a good member of anything, you have to be willing to do certain things. But a baby cannot promise to do the things that will make him a good member of the Church. Somebody else has to make the promises for him.

The Prayer Book states that when possible there are to be three godparents: for a boy, two godfathers and one godmother; for a girl, two godmothers and a godfather. (Page 273) It also says that parents may act as godparents.

If you look in the Prayer Book, pages 276–277, you will see that godparents make two kinds of promises in the baptismal service: they make certain promises *for their god-child,* and they promise *for themselves* that as he grows up they will help him to understand and keep these promises.

Godparents are meant to be a child's special friends in the Church. The Church means a great deal to them, and their godchild means a great deal to them. For example, many godparents take notice of the child's birthdays and also remember the anniversaries of his baptism, his birthday in the Church family. Because the Church is important to his godparents, who love him, it will also become important to the child.

Like the child, godparents will look forward to the day when he is old enough to study for confirmation. They, too, will be pleased and happy the day their godchild walks up to the chancel rail along with others to be confirmed. And they will probably be saying, silently along with the bishop, his prayer as he puts his hands on their godchild's head: "Defend, O Lord, this thy Child [and mine!] with thy heavenly grace; that he may continue thine for ever; and daily increase in thy Holy Spirit more and more, until he come unto thy everlasting kingdom. Amen." (Prayer Book, page 297)

Suggestions for further reading

The Hymnal: 186.

Other articles: Acceptance, Baptism, Church, Confirmation, Creed, Holy Communion, Holy Spirit, Sacrament.

Questions

Who are your godparents? What can *you* do to make this a happy relationship? If you were a godparent, what would you do for your godchild?

GOOD
is that which agrees with God's purpose

IF YOU WANTED TO DRIVE A NAIL into a wall, and picked up a screw driver and tried to hit the nail hard enough to make it go into the wood, you would very soon throw the screw driver aside and say, "I can't use that; it's no good!" This would mean that it was no good *as a hammer*. And this tells us one of the meanings of the word *good:* "to be able to carry out the intended purpose."

In the life of a person who is a Christian, goodness always means being good *for* something and *to* somebody. It does not mean just keeping out of mischief or doing nothing for fear of doing the wrong thing. It means being a good brother or sister, a good husband or wife, a good friend or neighbor, a good workman or employer, a good teacher or pupil. Goodness is always a matter of how people deal with each other; sometimes, how groups deal with groups. Humanly speaking, there is no such thing as private goodness or goodness all by itself. This is because we belong to each other and make up a family of God. All our human goodness is made possible by God's love for us.

Another part of the meaning of *good* is to be "true to one's promise." Sometimes a store claims that the quality of the things it sells is "as advertised." That is, the store lives up to its word. They say their shoes are good, and the shoes *are* good. The same idea is involved when the word is used to describe a check. When you ask, "Is the check good?" you mean, "Is there any money in the bank which can be used in the way the check says it can?" If there is, the check will be honored.

God does not go around with a record book jotting

down every little deed, putting this one down in the "Good" column, that one in the "Bad" column, and adding them up each day to see whether you are doing more harm than good. Instead, He knows *you*. And He always works to help you become the kind of person who will carry out His purpose.

Suggestions for further reading

The Hymnal: 519.
Other articles: Apostle, Christian, Conscience, Disciple, Kingdom of God, Obey, Right.

Questions

What are the differences in good for something, a good-for-nothing, and a goody-goody?

GOOD FRIDAY
*is the day on which we commemorate
the crucifixion of Jesus*

THE LAST WEEK OF LENT, Holy Week, is the time when the Church commemorates the events in the last week of our Lord's life on earth. Following the Last Supper on Thursday evening, Jesus and His disciples went out of Jerusalem to the garden of Gethsemane where He was arrested by Temple guards late in the evening. During the midnight hours Jesus was questioned by the high priest and members of the Sanhedrin. Early Friday morning he was taken to Pontius Pilate, the governor, who held court and sentenced Jesus to be crucified. According to an ancient tradition, when Jesus was crucified there was a darkness over the whole land from noon until three o'clock, when He died. Before six o'clock the body had been removed from the cross and buried in a tomb which belonged to Joseph of Arimethea.

All four Gospels tell these events in great detail: St. Matthew 26–27, St. Mark 14–15, St. Luke 22–23, St. John 18–19. These accounts are the appointed Gospels for Holy Week services.

The Church commemorates Good Friday with services in which the crucifixion story is heard, and frequently there are meditations or addresses on the meaning of Jesus' death. Often the meditations are based on the words spoken by Jesus from the cross. These "Seven Last Words," as they are called, are:

"Father, forgive them; for they know not what they do." (Luke 23:34, the Gospel for Maundy Thursday)

"Today shalt thou be with me in paradise." (Luke 23:43, the Gospel for Maundy Thursday)

"Woman, behold thy son!" "Behold thy mother!" (John 19:26–27, the Gospel for Good Friday)

"My God, my God, why hast thou forsaken me?" (Mark 15:34, the Gospel for the Tuesday before Easter)

"I thirst." (John 19:28, the Gospel for Good Friday)

"It is finished." (John 19:30, the Gospel for Good Friday)

"Father, into thy hands I commend my spirit." (Luke 23:46, the Gospel for Maundy Thursday)

Suggestions for further reading

The Hymnal: 65, 82.

Other articles: Atonement, Calvary.

Questions

Why is Good Friday called *good?*

THE GOSPEL

is the good news that God so loved us
He came to us in Christ

GOOD *news* is unexpected, or it would not be news. It is a happy surprise, or it would not be *good* news. If I have lost my bicycle and am worried about what my parents will think, it's good news to find out that they love me even though they are displeased with what I have done.

Good news makes a difference to us. It tells us something we did not know. Because we are glad to know about it, we change our plans. Instead of hiding the truth from my parents and pretending the bicycle is not lost, I can now go to them and we can plan together how it can be replaced.

The good news of the Gospel is that God did something new and that it is a wonderful thing. We can best find out about it in the four books called the Gospels. They tell the story of how God's love was made known to us in the life, death, and resurrection of Jesus Christ. We read about the things He did and said in the Gospels According to St. Matthew, St. Mark, St. Luke, and St. John. They are not biographies of Jesus, but they tell us how we can know who He was and how we can receive God's grace. Jesus is the good news that God loves us and will always love us, even though we fail Him and hurt each other.

85

Whenever the early Christians met for services, they used to recall things that Jesus had said or done. At first there were always people present who had seen or heard Him. But with the passage of time, these stories had to be written down. The Christians of later years had not known Jesus at first hand. The things the apostles and others remembered about Jesus are recorded in the Gospels. These records do not tell us everything Jesus did, but they tell us enough so that we know what the good news is.

The Gospels of SS. Matthew, Mark, and Luke are called the Synoptic Gospels because they follow the same arrangement or *synopsis* of events in the life and work of Jesus Christ.

We follow the custom of the early Church at the Holy Communion when we call one of the Bible lessons the Holy Gospel. It is a high point of the service, because in it we hear something that Jesus said or did.

THE GRACE OF GOD
is His freely given, saving power at work in the world and in us

ONE DAY A MOTHER hugged her little girl and said, "That is because you were so brave at the dentist's this morning." A few hours later she hugged the child and said, "This is because you helped me with the dishes." In the evening she gave the child still another hug. "What is that for?" asked the little girl. "Nothing," answered the mother. "It's just because I love you."

That was the most important hug of all. It wasn't *for* anything—except "for free." It was unearned. And this is the kind of love God has for every one of us. His loving-kindness to us is given freely, not in payment for anything we have done for Him. This is what we mean by God's *grace*.

The Bible says a great deal about this grace which God shows toward us and gives to us. We understand the grace of God better when we think of it in three ways.

The first meaning of the grace of God is the undeserved love and favor Almighty God offers to men. God chose the Israelites to be His special people, not because they had done wonderful things, but because He loved them. Having chosen them, He firmly refused to give them up. Bad as they were at times, God loved them so much that He would not give up His plan for them. He had made a covenant (an agreement) with them, and the covenant itself was an act of His grace. Through the years God's grace continued to be offered to His people in spite of their disobedience.

We can appreciate the wonderful nature of this kind of treatment because of what happens to us at home some-times. A boy (or girl) forgets a rule, perhaps because he loses his temper. He does something he knows his parents have forbidden him to do. They may even have punished him for doing it. This time it seems too much, and he feels like running away or giving up the struggle to be good. Perhaps he feels that he ought to be punished, and yet he couldn't seem to help doing what he did. It all seems hope-less. "What's the use?" he thinks. "I wish I were dead. I wish everybody would go away and never come back!" But what happens? His parents put their arms around him and show that they love him anyway. Although they know he did something wrong, they are patient and understanding. At cost to themselves, they stand by him. This is the way God treats us all. This is usually the meaning of *grace* when we find the word in the Old Testament—God's undeserved love and favor.

The second meaning of grace is familiar to us in the words "the grace of our Lord Jesus Christ." God shows His special love and favor to us through all that Jesus Christ was and said, through all that He did, and all that happened to Him. This meaning lies behind the words, "And the Word became flesh and dwelt among us, full of grace and truth; we have beheld his glory, glory as of the only Son from the Father." (John 1:14)

Since Jesus died on the Cross and rose from the dead, the grace of God is plainer than ever before. It shows the depth and wonder of God's love—the same love of the very same God who had chosen Israel and had been so patient through the long years before Christ came. In Jesus Christ we see the special love and favor God has toward us.

The third meaning of God's grace is that God's love and kindness are working inwardly in our hearts. By God's grace we are given power to act in ways acceptable to Him. In many of our prayers we ask God to give us grace to resist temptation and to do His will. These are prayers for God's power, for His Spirit, to work through our lives. Sometimes God's grace is known to us through the love and help of people around us. Our parish, with its worship and fellowship, is a place where this can take place. One of the chief ways in which God gives us indwelling power is through the sacraments. That is why they are called the "means of grace."

Suggestions for further reading

The Hymnal: 265, 524.

The Book of Common Prayer: pages 90, 109, 163, 204.

Other articles: Calvary, Conscience, Covenant, Cross, Faith, God, Holy Spirit, Love, Redemption.

Questions

What do we mean by the words *graceful, gracious,* and *full of grace?* Can we resist God's grace? In the Collect on page 214 of the Prayer Book, what is meant by *grace?*

H

TO HALLOW
means to make holy or sacred

WHEN WE SAY, "Hallowed be thy Name," we ask that God's Name be used only in a sacred or holy way. We ask that all God's words and works be treated with respect and held in reverence. All these words—*hallowed, sacred, holy, revered*—have to do with setting something apart as special, to keep it from being used in an ordinary way. After a building that is to be used for a church has been completed, even if it is very small and plain, special prayers are said in it to hallow it. (Prayer Book, pages 563–568) We ask God to set it apart as something holy, making it special as a place in which to worship Him. We also ask God to bless other things, such as the ring in a wedding (Prayer Book, page 302), because matrimony is holy, and the ring is a sign of the promises made by the husband and wife.

All Saints' Day has also been called Allhallows' Day, because the word *saint* means "holy." Therefore, All Saints' Eve, the day before All Saints' Day, was called Allhallows' Eve, and that was shortened to Halloween.

Suggestions for further reading
The Hymnal: 273.
Other articles: Name, Saint.

HEAVEN
is being so close to God that we know
and love Him perfectly

IN THE BIBLE we read many passages which tell us about heaven. Sometimes they speak of a beautiful city where everybody is happy because everybody is with God and serves Him gladly. The hymns also picture heaven. Sometimes people think of heaven as being like a great musical concert in which every member of the orchestra knows and plays his part perfectly under the direction of a great conductor.

If the descriptions you have read about heaven don't thrill you, just remember that they have to be in picture language, because nobody on earth has ever actually seen or heard the things that God has prepared for those who love Him. Heaven itself must be something so wonderful that it sweeps us off our feet—something "out of this world."

Being near God is like being near a friend. God is our friend, and He helps us to know and love Him now so that sometime we can know and love Him fully. We have to grow toward that closeness both in this life and the next, just as we have to grow in friendship with people now.

God loves all men. For His sake, because we love Him, we try to love the countless other people He loves. In the closeness to God which we call heaven, we shall love others perfectly and thus be close to them as well.

When you think of heaven, think of the best people and finest things you know. Heaven is like that. Above all, think of heaven as being with God as He has shown Himself to us in Jesus Christ. He is Perfect Love, and He will give us all the joy and happiness we could ever possibly want. He will come as close to us as we are willing to let Him.

Suggestions for further reading

The Hymnal: 586, 592.

Other articles: Judgment, Resurrection.

Questions

How does heaven begin on earth? Why don't most descriptions of heaven fully satisfy people?

HELL
is locking God out forever

Hell IS THE WORD the Bible uses to describe what it means to keep God out of our lives. If somebody always chose to do that, God simply could not get in, for God always respects our right to choose.

The pictures about hell which you sometimes find in the Bible talk about unending fire and similar torments. This is picture language. It is a way of saying that because God made us to live with Him, now and hereafter, it must be a terribly painful thing to be without His friendship forever. We can have a taste of hell even now if we go off by ourselves and sulk or refuse to make up after a quarrel.

Is there anybody in hell? Has anybody ever locked God out, once and for all? The Church does not say; only God Himself can know that. We have a right to hope that everybody who has ever lived will somehow, by God's mercy, be won to the service and love of God. On the other hand, we must not think that we can "take it easy" and never bother about trying to know and love God right here and now. There is no guarantee that we will get another chance.

Of course, we may fail time and time again. But God still loves us and will keep on loving us. If there is anybody in hell, now or ever, it is not because God wanted it so, but because a child of God chose to have it that way.

We love God as we know Him in Christ not in order to avoid hell, but simply because God is God and we love Him for His own sake.

Suggestions for further reading

The Hymnal: 356.
Other articles: Heaven, Judgment.

HOLY COMMUNION
also called the Lord's Supper
is the Church's central act of worship

THE HOLY COMMUNION is one of the two sacraments our Lord commands us all to observe. It was begun by Him at the Last Supper, the night before He was crucified. The Holy Communion is a family meal of the Lord's people at the Lord's table. It is the same service which is often called the Divine Liturgy, the Holy Eucharist, the Mass, the Holy Ordinance.

Jesus always used simple ideas to explain His teaching. (See "Parable.") In the Holy Communion He also used simple acts to do something important.

Everybody uses bread every day. In many countries wine is still the common drink, because no other drink is safe. So the bread and wine used in the Holy Communion stand for the food and drink without which no man can live. We cannot live as Christians without this strengthening and refreshing of our bodies and souls in the Sacrament of the Lord's Supper. When worshipers at the Lord's Supper kneel at the altar rail, they are coming in a very special way to receive into their lives the Lord Jesus Christ who gave Himself for the whole world.

In the service of Holy Communion we hear these words: "For in the night in which he was betrayed, he took Bread; and when he had given thanks, he brake it, and gave it to his disciples, saying, Take, eat, this is my Body, which is given for you; Do this in remembrance of me. Likewise, after supper, he took the Cup; and when he had given thanks, he gave it to them, saying, Drink ye all of this; for this is my Blood of the New Testament, which is shed for you, and for many, for the remission of sins; Do this, as oft as ye shall drink it, in remembrance of me."

In this sacrament the breaking of the bread stands for the sacrifice that Jesus made when He was crucified. We have to break bread in order to share it. So Christ's body was broken; He gave his life *for* us. He also shares His life *with* us. In the Holy Communion He comes to those who have faith in Him so that "we may evermore dwell in him, and he in us."

The sacrament is also the New Covenant. As the Offices of Instruction state it, "The Sacrament of the Lord's Supper was ordained for the continual remembrance of the sacrifice of the death of Christ, and of the benefits which we receive thereby." (Page 293) When we receive the cup, God renews the covenant He made with us at our baptism. God in Christ gives Himself to us so that we may give ourselves to Him. He draws us to Himself so that we can be a part of His perfect offering. Thus we share in the worship of the whole "company of heaven."

The sacrament has been called the Eucharist (Prayer Book, page 574) because *eucharist* means "thanksgiving." This note runs through the whole service. We are chiefly thankful for God's coming to us as man in Christ—the great gift of God the Father on the first Christmas. The only way we can respond is thankfully to present ourselves as His guests, trusting in His promise to be there to meet us.

> "He was the Word, that spake it:
> He took the bread and brake it;
> And what that Word did make it,
> I do believe and take it."

Suggestions for further reading

The Hymnal: 189, 199, 201, 211.
Other articles: Covenant, Kingdom of God, Sacrament.

Questions

There are various ways to understand the presence of our Lord in this sacrament. Ask your priest to discuss this point with you.

What should you do to prepare yourself for receiving

Holy Communion? Why does the Episcopal Church consider the service of Holy Communion very important? In what way can your family meals at home be a sort of communion? What is the connection between our offering of money and our offering of the bread and wine?

HOLY DAYS
are special days in the Church Year dedicated to a saint or to some event in our Lord's life

THE HOLY DAYS USED TO BE the only holidays working people had. On holy days they had such a good time, we use the name for our days of rest and recreation.

Saints' days usually commemorate the death and martyrdom of a godly person—that is, his birthday into Eternal Life. These days started as observances of the martyrdom of a Christian. They were celebrated in the place where he had lived, by the people who still lived there, to honor the way he lived and the spirit in which he had died. His life and death were an inspiration to his fellow Churchman. In time, as the fame of the local saint spread, his day was celebrated in other communities. The Book of Common Prayer commemorates only persons mentioned in the New Testament.

The other holy days in the Prayer Book are feasts of our Lord. These are the Circumcision of Christ, the Presentation of Christ in the Temple, the Annunciation of the blessed Virgin Mary, and the Transfiguration of Christ.

The Prayer Book calendar of holy days is found on pages xlvi–xlix.

THE HOLY SPIRIT OR HOLY GHOST
*is God as He gives life to all things
and holiness to people*

A FOOTBALL TEAM MAY HAVE a good spirit, but we refer to team spirit as "it." The Holy Spirit is "He." He works among us in the life of the Church. He is "The Lord, and Giver of Life . . . Who spake by the Prophets." When we speak of the Holy Spirit (*Ghost* is the Anglo-Saxon word for "spirit"), we mean God just as much as when we talk about God the Father or Jesus Christ our Lord. He is active and living. Since the Holy Spirit is God, He is personal. He guides and inspires the Christian Church.

1. *The Holy Spirit dwells in the Church.* The followers of our Lord were meeting together in a group when they first knew they had been given God's Spirit. (See Acts 2:1-4.) This was true of the early Church over and over: when those who looked to Jesus as their risen Lord were together, their worshiping fellowship was blessed by the presence of God the Holy Spirit. (See Acts 4:31 and 10:44-48.) This has been the experience of the Christian Church ever since. In the Christian Church we believe the Holy Spirit blesses and sanctifies all sacramental acts. He binds the Church's members together, inspires them, and guides them not only as they act together but as they go forth to act separately in God's name.

2. *The Holy Spirit inspires people.* He inspired the prophets of the Old Testament and the other writers of the Bible. He is God's active power in giving life. "The Lord, and Giver of Life," we say in the Nicene Creed. He inspires those poets, artists, sculptors, and musicians who strive to give expression to God's truth. He works through

the lives of brave men and women who fight for right and justice with pen and word and sword as writers, statesmen, and soldiers. He speaks through the consciences of those who try humbly, as members of the Christian fellowship, to obey Him. He never tells us to think or do anything which is not according to Christ's will.

3. *The Holy Spirit helps us become saints.* Just as a person's daily living should reflect the spirit of his family, so a member of the Church should reflect the Holy Spirit. The New Testament calls Church members *saints*, meaning "holy ones," because in their lives the work of the Holy Spirit can be seen.

The Christlike qualities in individual Church members are called by St. Paul "the fruit of the Spirit." This is what the Prayer Book means when it says on page 285 that the Holy Ghost "sanctifieth me, and all the people of God." The word *sanctify* means "make holy," and to be holy is to be whole or healthy in spirit.

4. *The Holy Spirit blesses things.* He hallows such things as the water of Holy Baptism, the bread and wine of Holy Communion, the oil for the anointing of the sick, the ring in Holy Matrimony.

Even if we do recognize the presence of the Holy Spirit, we must not assume we can know all about Him. We can be sure, however, that He always works for good and to bring us closer to God in Christ.

Suggestions for further reading

The Hymnal: 217, 243, 370, 477.

Other articles: Fellowship, Pentecost, Sacrament, Sanctify, Trinity.

Questions

How can you tell when your hunch or urge to do something is probably from the Holy Spirit? What do we mean by *sacramental acts?*

I

AN IMAGE
is a copy which is like the thing itself

THE BIBLE TEACHES US that man was made "in the image of God." (Gen. 1:27) This does not mean that we are God, or even that we look like God. God has never been seen. It means that there is something about our life that is like God's life. We are meant to be His children and to grow to be like Him.

If you look in a mirror, you see a reflection of yourself. It is not you, but it is exactly like you. If you press a seal into warm wax, there will be an exact copy of the seal when the wax hardens. But it is not the seal. The film in a camera will give an exact picture of what was in the field of the lens. When you look at the print, you may see something you did not see when you took the picture.

If the mirror in which you look is cracked or twisted, the reflection will not look much like you. You can have fun looking in such mirrors at a fair, but you would not want to look like *that*. The image of the seal will not be perfect if there is a hard lump in the wax or someone pushes it about while it is still soft. So the Bible tells us the image of God in man was twisted or "defected" by sin. We cannot tell by looking at other people exactly what we were supposed to be like.

Then God sent His only Son, Jesus, to show us what He Himself is like. Jesus is called "the image of the invisible God." (Col. 1:15) By looking at a picture, you can see a place where you have never been. By looking at Jesus, at His way of living and loving, and by listening to His words, we can tell what God always meant us to be. As we become more and more like Jesus, the image of God begins to come clear in us again. The more like Jesus we are, the more people can see in us a little of Christ, the true image or reflection of God.

Jesus is the only true Son of God because He is completely like His Father in heaven. We were marked with the Cross as God's children at baptism. We are intended to grow into the likeness of the Son of God.

In the First Epistle of St. John there is a description of God's plan for us: "Beloved, we are God's children now; it does not yet appear what we shall be, but we know that when he appears we shall be like him, for we shall see him as he is." (I John 3:2)

Suggestions for further reading

The Hymnal: 404, 414, 418.
Other articles: The Fall.

Questions

Have you an "ideal," someone you want to be like? Does who he or she is make a difference to the way you behave?

THE INCARNATION
means that God the Son became man

Two boys were looking at a picture of Babe Ruth, the great home-run hitter. "He was the greatest player of all," said one. "Yes, I know," said the other. "I wish I could have seen him in person—*in the flesh*." The word *incarnation* means "being in the flesh." *The* Incarnation means more than this.

God the Son, together with the Father and the Holy Spirit, has existed always. But, as God, He is invisible. Therefore no one could see Him *in the flesh* until He came to us as Jesus more than nineteen hundred years ago. He did not stop being God, but from then on He has been God *and* man, both at the same time.

God came to us in Jesus Christ to show us what He really is and to make us one with Him. We see in Jesus a full and perfect man, but He is also incarnate God. And "Whoever confesses that Jesus is the Son of God, God abides in him, and he in God." (I John 4:15)

It took even His disciples a long time to see that. At first they thought Jesus was just a wonderful man and nothing more. But the better they knew Him, the more they felt a strange sense of awe. He made their consciences work. He made them want to get down on their knees. A man once said, "If Shakespeare should come into the room, I would rise. If Jesus should come into the room, I would fall on my knees." That was how the disciples felt. Yet still they did not see the full truth.

Christ's death on the Cross was a terrible shock to His disciples. But on the third day He rose again. He invited them to touch Him. They saw Him eat. He spoke familiar words to them. Then at last the truth dawned on them. Thomas looked at Jesus and said, "My Lord and my God."

The risen Christ lives with us in this world and gives us His love. Our need is to know Him. We cannot understand completely the mystery of the Incarnation, though we learn as much as we can in the Bible and in church. Christ still makes Himself known to us in the breaking of bread. When we try to live the way Christ wants us to, we find that He helps us. We find that we are truly children of God and that we have the power to respond to the love of God in Christ.

So we do not have to guess what God is like. We do not have to guess whether God loves us. For the Jesus who is really man, who was born in a stable, died on a cross, and came back from death to seek for us and save us— this Jesus is also truly God. That is what we say in the Nicene Creed: that Jesus Christ our Lord is "God of God, Light of Light, Very God of very God."

Suggestions for further reading

The Hymnal: 12, 20, 41, 239, 344.
Other articles: Atonement, God, Holy Spirit, Image, Reconciliation, Redemption, Resurrection, Trinity.

AN INHERITOR
*is one who receives a gift or responsibility
through an arrangement made beforehand by the giver*

YOU ARE AN HEIR if you receive money or anything else from a person who leaves a gift to you in his will. If you take over benefits or responsibilities from a person who held them just before you, you are like a president who inherits the duties of his office from his predecessor.

Inheritors of the kingdom of heaven have received the Kingdom as a gift prepared for them by God. You received membership in it when you were baptized. All your life you have to decide again and again whether you will live as a member of it.

Jesus told of people who fed the hungry, were good to strangers, visited the sick. He said that God would say to them, "Come . . . inherit the kingdom prepared for you from the foundation of the world." (Matt. 25:34)

The whole matter is well summed up in the Collect on page 197 of the Prayer Book:

"O God, who hast prepared for those who love thee such good things as pass man's understanding; Pour into our hearts such love toward thee, that we, loving thee above all things, may obtain thy promises, which exceed all that we can desire. . . ."

Suggestions for further reading

Other articles: Grace, Kingdom of God.

Questions

What are the privileges of being an inheritor of the kingdom of heaven? What are the responsibilities? Think how you and your church school class can feed the hungry, be good to strangers, and visit the sick.

J

JESUS
is our Lord's human name

Let us look at Jesus. "He was born in an obscure village, the child of a peasant woman. He grew up in another obscure village. He worked in a carpenter shop until He was thirty. Then for a year or so He was a wandering preacher. He never wrote a book. He never held an office.

"He never owned a home. He never set foot inside a city bigger than Jerusalem. He never traveled two hundred miles from the place where He was born. He had no credentials but Himself.

"He had nothing to do with this world except the simple power of His divine manhood. While still a young man, the tide of popular opinion turned against Him. His friends ran away. One of them denied Him. He was turned over to His enemies. He went through the mockery of a trial. He was nailed upon a cross between two thieves.

"His executioners gambled for the only piece of property He had on earth when He was dying—and that was His coat. When He was dead He was taken down and laid in a borrowed grave through the pity of a friend.

"Nineteen wide centuries have come and gone and today He is the centerpiece of the human race and the Savior of mankind. I am far within the mark when I say that all the armies that ever marched, and all the navies that ever were built, and all the parliaments that ever sat, and all the kings that ever reigned, put together, have not affected the life of man upon earth as powerfully as the One Solitary Life."[1]

Suggestions for further reading

The Hymnal: 323, 346, 352, 455.

Other articles: Atonement, Christ, Christmas Day, Incarnation, Redemption.

THE JUDGMENT OF GOD
is His evaluation of us in absolute fairness and love

GOD KNOWS OUR DEEPEST SECRETS, good and bad. He not only knows what we do, but why we do it. God does not look the other way when we do wrong so that He can let us off. If He did, He would not be very much interested in us. He would not be doing the best thing for us. Even a human father learns that if he is never firm with his children, he does them harm. This kind of concern over our behavior is what the judgment of God means.

God is not just righteous, He is Righteousness. Every thing, every thought that is good and true and fine, shows something of God. When we think or do a bad thing, God

---

[1] "One Solitary Life," author unknown. Quoted from *The Reader's Notebook* by Gerald Kennedy and used by permission of Bishop Kennedy and Harper & Brothers, New York.

sees that it is bad. He doesn't make it out to be worse than it really is, nor does He pretend that it is not really wrong. He judges the wrong deed, and because He is God, He also judges us.

Even the best and finest people in the world stand under God's judgment. Every minute of the day we do, too, but we need not be afraid, because we know that He loves us. His love is so serious and so deep that it will not stand any "fooling."

When you are playing a game, every point you make counts, but there comes a time when the game is over and the final score is announced. It's something like that with us. Some day there will be the final score. When the Church talks about the "Last Judgment" it means that some time or other God has to make a final evaluation of us. We can trust Him to be absolutely fair and absolutely loving. He now does all He can to help us, and He will keep on doing so. He will take account of every single good thing we have done, and what we meant when we did it. He will not overlook anything that is good in us. The real question is: have we accepted His love and forgiveness? *Now* is the time for us to make up our minds about this. In that sense, *every* day is judgment day and the *last* judgment is the announcement of the final score.

Suggestions for further reading

The Hymnal: 518, 538.
Other articles: Heaven, Hell, Second Coming.

Questions

We have learned that God is Love and that He is our Judge. Is one aspect more important than the other? What would our religion be like if God were not a judge? Or if He were not Love?

JUSTIFICATION BY FAITH
is God's acceptance of us as soon as we trust Him

SOME RELIGIONS TELL US, "Do what is good and what is right, *then* God will welcome you." This means the welcome is earned. It is bought with one's goodness. As Christians, we believe that we have a different kind of relationship with God: justification by God's grace through faith.

The word *justify*, from which *justification* comes, means "to make just," "to put right." We cannot put ourselves in the right with God by doing good deeds. We are always sinners: "We have left undone those things which we ought to have done; And we have done those things which we ought not to have done. . . ."

But Christians believe that Christ died on the Cross so that we could be forgiven. We can be forgiven as soon as we really trust Him. Then we try to show our gratitude by being the kind of person God wants us to be. God treats us *as if* we were upright, and this helps us to become right with Him and with other people. When a friend loves me as I am now, but treats me as if I were finer and more upright than I am, he is actually helping me to become a finer person. That is the way God's gift of grace and forgiveness works.

I have not earned God's love, but whenever I realize that I have received His gift of grace and forgiveness, and respond to it, God helps me to live according to His will.

Suggestions for further reading

The Hymnal: 337, 409.

Other articles: Atonement, Faith, Grace, Obey, Reconciliation, Redemption.

Questions

Why can't we *earn* our way into the Kingdom by being good? If we can't earn our way into the Kingdom, why should we try to be good?

K

THE KINGDOM OF GOD
is God's rule through Christ

AT THE TIME Jesus lived, a king was in complete control of his subjects. A good king was like a shepherd; he cared about his people and looked after them. A king is not elected as a president is. Nor do we elect God king. He is always King. It is sensible and right that He should rule because He created everything and knows how it should work. We have only to accept His rule and things will be as He planned them. Nothing that works against God's rule can ever last.

God's people, the Jews, always dreamed of a time when He would rule over all men. At first they thought His rule would come through the King of Israel. When things got worse, they looked for a king from heaven. He would be sent by God and would be anointed by Him as a king was anointed. So they called him "Messiah," which means "anointed."

Then Jesus came. He said, "The time is fulfilled, and the kingdom of God is at hand; repent, and believe in the gospel." (Mark 1:15) Where He went, wonderful things began to happen. The sick were healed, lepers were cleansed, demons were cast out. His teaching had an authority that amazed people. When they responded, they found that they could live together. Where Jesus was, the power and love of God were at work in a new way.

But Jesus did not look like a king: He looked like a baby, then like a carpenter at his bench—a neighbor in Nazareth. So, many people did not accept Him as king.

Even though people did not realize it, the kingdom of God was near when Jesus came. This is true now. Where Christ touches life, this same new power of good is at work. He helps us to live together. Through Christ, God's victory over sin and evil has been won.

Jesus taught us to pray, "Thy kingdom come." His prayer asks that Christ's power over men be spread until all accept Him as their Lord. Then He can present His kingdom to God. God has always ruled and always will, but the Kingdom will not come for us until we accept Jesus as the King whom God has sent. He is the King, but we must give Him our allegiance.

We cannot build or make the Kingdom. God gives it to us in Christ. It is like a harvest which has to be gathered when it is ready. We can prepare its way; we can do its work in the world. Each of us, by God's grace, entered the Kingdom when he was baptized. We can pray for it to come more and more into our own lives and into the world's life.

We experience the Kingdom in the Church. In the life of the Church where Christ is worshiped and his ways are accepted, we have a preview of what the Kingdom will finally be like. But we cannot fully know what it is until the day when God takes the whole world into the Kingdom of Christ.

Suggestions for further reading

The Hymnal: 350, 351, 536, 538, 545.
Other articles: Baptism, Christ, Inheritor.

Questions

How do we keep God's kingdom from coming? Why do Christians talk about the Kingdom rather than the Republic of God or the Democracy of God, with God as president? What do the parables tell us that begin, "The kingdom of God [or heaven] is like . . ."?

L

THE LAW
is the term for the commandments God gave His people

IN THE TWENTIETH CHAPTER of Exodus we read the Hebrew story of how God gave the Law to Moses. On the mountaintop, amid "the thunderings and the lightnings and the sound of the trumpet and the mountain smoking," Moses received from God the Ten Commandments.

There was more to ancient Jewish law than these ten commandments, however. There were rules about ceremonies and tribal and personal actions which had little to do with the great commands. Ever since the time of Moses, the Ten Commandments have been the basic moral law for Jews and Christians.

Chapter 22 of the Gospel According to St. Matthew gives us another picture. Jesus was talking with some Jews who had come to test His teaching. One of them asked Him, "Teacher, which is the great commandment in the law?" And Jesus answered, "You shall love the Lord your God with all your heart, and with all your soul, and with all your mind. This is the great and first commandment. And a second is like it, You shall love your neighbor as yourself." Then he added, "On these two commandments depend all the law and the prophets."

From the ancient chosen people of God we get the Law. From Jesus we learn how we should obey the Law.

The Ten Commandments set the boundary within which we should live. Our Lord, in the summary of the Law, tells us that back of all God's commandments is His love. He loves us, so we should love and obey Him and learn to love all people whom He has made. Our Lord said, "A new commandment I give to you, that you love one another." (John 13:34) If we, as Christians, are to love God and obey Him, we are also bound to love our neighbors—our parents, teachers, and those who enforce the law —and to obey their just commands. Human laws can be unjust and bad; if they are, we should, as citizens, seek to change them. But God's law is eternal, and His command to love is eternal, too.

Suggestions for further reading

The Hymnal: 515, 523.
Other articles: Conscience, Judgment, Obey.

Questions

What laws are hardest for you to keep? If you were driving, and there were no one in sight anywhere, what would be wrong with going through a stop sign? Why do personal relationships often involve more injured feelings than broken laws do?

A LAYMAN
in the Church is a member of God's people

WHEN A CHRISTIAN IS BAPTIZED, he is made a member of the Church, which is the community of the Covenant. As the Jew is a member of Israel, so the Christian is a member of the new Israel, of which Jesus Christ is Lord and Head.

To be a layman means to have special responsibilities, as well as privileges. It means to serve and follow Christ, and to live as He would have us live. And it means that we have a real ministry in the Church.

There are various kinds of ministry. There is the ordained ministry, which includes bishops, priests, and deacons. And there is also the ministry or priesthood of the laity. ". . . You are a chosen race, a royal priesthood," we read in I Peter 2:9. In confirmation, a layman receives additional strength from the Holy Spirit to enable him to carry out his responsibilities as a member of the lay ministry.

A layman has his own part and place in the worship of the Church. For instance, he says the responses, he joins in the hymns, he may assist as server and chorister. But he also has his own work in the Church. In his own place in life he is a witness to Christ, just as much as a clergyman is in his. How he lives and what he says have an effect on his friends and neighbors. How he behaves in his family shows how seriously he takes his faith.

Suggestions for further reading

The Hymnal: 524, 533, 576.

Other articles: Apostle, Disciple, Minister, Mission, Vocation, Witness.

Questions

Can you baptize a baby? Can you conduct Morning Prayer? When does one become a layman?

LENT

consists of the forty weekdays before Easter

LENT ALMOST ALWAYS comes at the time baseball players go south or west for spring training. When the warm weather comes, players start exercising in order to loosen their muscles. They practice throwing, fielding, and batting. After about six weeks they are in good shape for the beginning of the baseball season.

So it is with Lent. This is the Church's spring training season. Only those who get in shape are ready to appreciate Easter, for those who give the most get the most from the great climax of the Christian Year at Easter. In the early Church, Lent was often the period of preparation for baptism on Easter Even, and it still is in mission fields.

When you train yourself for Christian living, you begin by getting yourself under control so that you can live under God's rule. You become an athlete of the spirit. (See I Cor. 9:24–27.) One way you can do this is by fasting. You give up something you like (such as candy, gum, sodas, desserts, movies) because you want to. But you don't stop there. You take the money saved and put it in your Church School Missionary Offering box. Or you use the time gained to do something extra for your parents or for the Church. Perhaps you read a book on religion or attend extra Church services.

You become a better Christian during Lent if you do these things *on your own*. If you do them because someone tells you, that is better than nothing. But if you learn to make your own decisions, you become stronger in your own faith. *Self*-control is the key.

The forty days of Lent are based on the story of the forty days Jesus spent in the wilderness when He was tempted. He was training for His special task.

Throughout Lent you should keep the climax of Holy Week and Easter in mind. In your imagination, you ride into Jerusalem with Jesus on Palm Sunday, visit the Temple with Him, share the Last Supper in the upper room, and watch the ugliness and tragedy of His trial and death. Only then do you understand the glory of Easter.

Lent gets you ready: (1) to understand that life is not all play and having your own way; (2) to know that God triumphs; (3) to be a better servant of God in His victory; (4) to have a stronger will to be a Christian *all year long;* (5) to win a victory over sin.

Suggestions for further reading

The Hymnal: 55, 61, 68.
Other articles: Discipline, Fasting, Temptation.

Questions

Plan a rule for yourself for Lent. What things have you *added* to your normal schedule? One boy said that he was going to give up soup for Lent because he didn't like it anyhow. Whose way was he following?

A LITANY

*is a public prayer in dialogue form
said by minister and people*

Litany IS A GREEK WORD which means "prayer." In English
a litany is a special kind of prayer. The leader says part of
each paragraph out loud, and the people of the congregation finish it out loud. The two parts are indicated by two
styles of type. Sometimes a whole service is made up of
this back-and-forth kind of prayer. In such a service there
are no canticles or lessons, although there may be appropriate hymns.

Sometimes a litany is sung, and often a choir helps the
congregation sing its part. Such a service may be sung in
procession as minister, choir, and congregation march up
and down the aisles of the church. The procession may also
be held out-of-doors through the streets, across fields, or
through gardens. Often an outdoor litany is a service asking
God to bless the crops and make them grow well or thank-
ing God for a good harvest. A litany, however, can be on
any subject. For example, on page 59 of the Prayer Book
there is a portion of a litany once used in time of war.

The Litany or General Supplication is the principle
service of this type in the Prayer Book, and it is the oldest
church service we have in English. It was first published
along with accompanying music in 1544. The first Book
of Common Prayer was not published until five years later,
1549.

The Litany which begins on page 54 has five parts: (1)
solemn addresses to the Holy Trinity; (2) petitions asking
that God deliver us from all evil; (3) prayers addressed to
our Lord in which we remember His saving acts on our

behalf; (4) a long series of intercessions which ends with a set of solemn addresses to our Lord and with the Lord's Prayer; (5) a closing section made up of versicles and collects.

One might think that a prayer as long as the Litany would be tiresome or monotonous. This is not the case. The back-and-forth sharing by congregation and minister, and the rhythmical quality of the phrases we repeat, seem to draw worshipers together. It is one of the most dearly loved of services.

Suggestions for further reading

The Book of Common Prayer: pages 317, 560.

The Hymnal: Litanies which may be sung or said, 180, 229–234. An appropriate hymn to use with the Litany, 332.

Other articles: Liturgy, Prayer, Rogation Days, Worship.

Questions

What are the advantages of this type of prayer? If you were to compose a litany, what things would you pray for?

LITURGY

*is the public worship of the Church shared in
by both minister and people*

A LITURGICAL SERVICE is written beforehand. It is planned and orderly, and it cannot properly be held unless both the leader and people take their respective parts. A prepared service makes it possible for everyone to take part intelligently without depending on instructions from the leader.

In any liturgical service the people, as well as the minister who leads the service, have a definite part to play. In our Prayer Book liturgy, the order in which the various parts of the service follow each other is decided in advance. Most of the words are always the same, too, though on different days we have different Bible lessons, and there are places where certain choices are given. Hymns and anthems are left to the minister to choose. In many parts of the services we are told to stand, sit, or kneel. Such actions are called *ceremonies*.

The early Christians chose the word *liturgy* to mean the public worship of the Church and the forms used in administering the sacraments. In our Church, liturgy usually means the services in the Prayer Book. (Notice the use of the word on page iv of the Prayer Book opposite the Preface.) In the Eastern Orthodox Churches "The Divine Liturgy" is the title for the Holy Communion.

Suggestions for further reading

The Hymnal: 160, 164, 171, 315.
Other articles: Holy Communion, Litany, Worship.

TO LOVE
is to care deeply

THE WORD *love* is used in many ways. At best it refers to a relationship that is fine and noble. The highest kind of love is a genuine, deep concern of one person for another, interest in his welfare, and a deep desire for his companionship. It involves something deeper than feeling. It makes you want to do something for the other's good.

We see love in many different relationships.

1. *The love of God for man*. The whole Bible tells the story of the yearning, caring, loving concern of God for His people. This is the "love that wilt not let me go" of which we read in Hymn 458. It is the love that we see in Jesus Christ: His coming, His life, His death. "For God so loved the world that he gave his only Son. . . ." (John 3:16) His love is so perfect that the Bible says, "God *is* love." (See Hymn 239.)

2. *The love of man for God*. This is our response to God's great love for us. "We love, because he first loved us." (I John 4:19) We show our love for Him by living with people around us as God wants us to and by worshiping Him with sincerity. (See Hymn 156.)

3. *The love of friend for friend*. If boys or girls are friends, they like to do kind and thoughtful things for each other. Sometimes one friend will suffer punishment rather than let the other one down. The book, *The Three Musketeers*, describes such a deep friendship. Many heroes on the battlefield have shown this kind of love. "Greater love has no man than this, that a man lay down his life for his friends." (John 15:13) This love may cause us pain, for as a friend there are times when we have to speak out when we see our friends doing something that hurts them or someone else badly. We may risk misunderstanding. (See Hymn 493.)

4. *The love of man and woman*. Many great stories describe the strength of the love between a man and a woman. It makes a bond between two people which produces a home in which children will be cared for and others will find a warm welcome. This is the love that the marriage service expects. (See Hymn 214.)

5. *The love of parent for child.* When a poet seeks to describe self-sacrificing love, he often writes about the tender love of a mother for her baby. Many times parents deny themselves to help their children, whom they dearly love. The Bible frequently describes God's love for His people in terms of a father's love for his children. (See Hymn 504.)

6. *The love of man for the unfortunate.* Jesus spent much time with the unpopular and outcast, the handicapped and sick. He accepted them as brothers. There was no question that He *ought* to help them out. He did it because He loved them. Albert Schweitzer shows this kind of love in Africa today. So did Florence Nightingale and many others. Jesus said that to be kind to another person is to be loving to God, and that to pay no attention to a needy person is to pay no attention to God. (Matt. 25:31–46) We learn from the Bible that the love people have for one another reflects the love God has for us and we for Him.

Suggestions for further reading

The Hymnal: 405, 498.

Other articles: Acceptance, Atonement, Forgiveness, Holy Matrimony.

M

HOLY MATRIMONY
is the lifelong union of a man and a woman as husband and wife

HOLY MATRIMONY, or Holy Wedlock, is marriage entered into with the protection and prayers and blessing of the Church. In the service of the Solemnization of Matrimony, the man and woman marry each other. But God binds them together in a union "so long as [they] both shall live."

Holy Matrimony is a sacramental rite of the Church. A clergyman presides over the wedding. He guides the man and the woman as they make their promises, each to the other. He also takes the ring and gives it to the man to put on the fourth finger of the woman's left hand. Before this he may bless the ring. The ring and the joining of hands are the symbols of the agreement they make with each other. At the end of the service, the minister makes a formal declaration that these two persons are now man and wife. Then he gives them God's blessing in order that they may "so live together in this life, that in the world to come [they] may have life everlasting." For those who wish to receive Communion on the day of their wedding, the Prayer Book provides a collect, epistle, and gospel (pages 267–268).

Before a marriage can be solemnized, the Church requires enough advance notice to the minister so that he can give the man and woman instruction in the nature of Christian matrimony.

Suggestions for further reading

The Book of Common Prayer: pages 300–304.

A MEDIATOR
is one who brings estranged persons together

WHEN TWO CHILDREN get into a hot argument, neither wants to understand the other. A teacher can sometimes help them settle the whole thing. When he does, the teacher is acting as a *mediator*. If the teacher is really successful, the argument will be settled, and the children will begin to understand each other.

Because Jesus is both God and man, He brings God and man together. Before He came, human sin had been keeping them apart. Jesus shared both God's and man's side, and so He was the only one who could bring the two together. But even He could not do this without the cost of complete sacrifice.

The big difference between the case of the two children and the relationship between God and man is that, though both children needed to be changed, only *man* needs changing. God does not change. He is perfect love and perfect righteousness, and He *sent* Christ.

Suggestions for further reading

The Hymnal: 267.

Other articles: Atonement, Incarnation, Reconciliation, Redemption, Saviour.

Questions

What are some ways that mediation is used today in the family? In labor relations? What does the word *Mediator* mean on page 18 in the Prayer Book?

MEMBER
see Church

MESSIAH
see Christ

A MINISTER
*is a man to whom God gives power and authority
to speak and act for Him*

THE WORD *minister* means "servant," and in the Book of Common Prayer it is used to refer to any person who acts for the Church. Such a person is usually ordained, but a bishop may license a layman to read some services. There are three orders of ordained ministers: bishops, priests, and deacons. All of these are ministers just as, in the army, all generals, colonels, majors, captains, and lieutenants are officers.

When you address a letter to a bishop, the proper form is "The Right Reverend George Smith." If you speak to him by name, you say "Bishop Smith." A letter to a priest or deacon should be addressed "The Reverend George Smith." If he is a priest, you may call him "Mr. Smith" or "Father Smith." If he is a deacon, you call him "Mr. Smith." If he has a doctor's degree, he may be called "Doctor Smith." It is *never* correct to refer to an ordained minister simply as "Reverend Smith."

In Christianity one is glad to be a servant. Jesus said to his disciples, ". . . let the greatest among you become as the youngest, and the leader as one who serves." (Luke 22:26) Greatness, in other words, is measured by willingness to serve. Jesus said of Himself that He "came not to be served but to serve [minister], and to give his life. . . ." (Matt. 20:28)

The idea of serving others—ministering to their needs—applies to us all. In this sense we are all ministers. God trusts us to do for each other even while we are children, and even in sacred things: by intercession, by giving alms, by singing in the choir, and in other ways. When a boy grows up, God may give him power to speak and act for Him as a deacon or a priest or a bishop. When a girl grows up God may trust her to be a teacher, a nurse, a missionary, a deaconess, or a sister. The great minister (servant of all) is Jesus Himself.

Suggestions for further reading

The Hymnal: 219, 220.
Other articles: Bishop, Deacon, Layman, Priest.

Questions

What is the difference in the meanings of the words

rector, preacher, pastor, minister, layman? Can you name some of the other ways in which people can minister for God in the Church?

THE MISSION OF THE CHURCH
is to carry the good news of Jesus Christ to everyone

JESUS SAID, "As the Father has sent me, even so I send you." (John 20:21) Jesus Himself is God's great missionary to mankind, and He sends all Christians to continue His work. So the Church has a world-wide mission.

There is no one on earth who does not need God. Everyone needs to know he belongs to God and that God cares for him. He needs to know Christ and to make Him known. One of the ways the Church shows people God's love for them is to put churches, ministers, teachers, hospitals, and schools wherever they are needed. The Church's mission is never finished.

The first thing the pioneers did when they climbed down from their covered wagons was to start a church. They were missionaries. Once missionaries brought the message of Jesus Christ to your town and started the churches there. If it were not for these people, you would not now have a church in which to pray, listen to preaching, and receive the sacraments. You can be thankful that missionaries brought the Gospel of Christ to the place where you live.

But it is not enough just to feel thankful. We must put our thankfulness to work by being missionaries ourselves. Love is different from most other things. *The more we give of it, the more we have.* All of us have the mission to let people see by our actions and our words that we love God and His Son Jesus Christ. This is *bearing witness*, and it helps the Church to grow.

You may decide some day to bear witness in some far-off country. You may decide to do it at home. You can be a missionary in the priesthood, in a business, as an engineer, a cowboy, a teacher, a trained nurse, or a fireman. No matter how you earn your living, you can be a missionary while you are doing it. All Church members are meant to be missionaries.

Suggestions for further reading

The Hymnal: 261, 262, 498.
Other articles: Apostle, Vocation, Witness.

Questions

Why is a Christian concerned about the needs of people in far-away places? Do you know any missionaries of the Episcopal Church in a foreign country? In our own land? In your city? In your class? Are there any opportunities for missionary work for you and your class *right now?*

MORNING AND EVENING PRAYER
are the Church's daily offering of prayer and praise

MORNING AND EVENING PRAYER are Bible-reading services and are very much alike. The point of either service is the reading of psalms and lessons from the Old and New Testaments. Through the Holy Scriptures, God Himself speaks to our hearts and minds. Something really happens between God and all who listen in faith. It is as if He touched you on the shoulder and said, "I have something to say to you."

After each lesson we respond with a canticle. Then we join in saying the Creed, a statement of beliefs based on what the Bible teaches. This is followed by a series of prayers.

Our Church often speaks of God's "Word and Sacraments." Some of the services in the Prayer Book are services of the Word; others are sacraments or sacramental rites. The principal "Word" service is Morning (or Evening) Prayer. The chief sacrament is the Holy Communion. In both types of service, God is the chief actor. Whether He comes through His Word or through His sacraments, He is the same God.

Suggestions for further reading

Other articles: Bible, Sacrament, Word of God.

TO MURDER
is to hate a person enough to kill him

"THOU SHALT DO NO MURDER" is the Sixth Commandment. God made every one of us. Therefore a person's life is of great value to God. Once it is taken away, it cannot be replaced by man.

Most of us think that this commandment has to do only with killing somebody. We say, "I'm no murderer, and I don't intend to be." In the Sermon on the Mount Jesus says we are all guilty if we commit murder in our hearts. (Matt. 5:21-26) No one is likely to say to himself, "I think I'll murder someone this afternoon." But we are likely to have a series of ill feelings about a person, each a little worse than the one before. For example:

"He always disagrees with me."

"I don't like people who disagree with me."

"He is just being mean."

"Oh, there is that spiteful guy again. I wish he'd get lost."

"I wish something would happen to him, like getting run over."

"Somebody ought to kill him. He deserves it."

Jesus taught His disciples that leaving people out, quarreling, holding grudges, hatefulness, nasty sneers, and spiteful name-calling break the Sixth Commandment in spirit if not in act. All of us realize that something is "killed" when acts like these make people feel rejected. One who breaks the commandment to love his neighbor as himself is in danger of breaking the Sixth Commandment also.

Suggestions for further reading

Other articles: Conscience, Law, Love, Rejection.

Questions

Why do we often find movies and television shows with a murder theme very exciting? How do the Offices of Instruction explain the Sixth Commandment? (Prayer Book, page 288.) Is it murder to kill to defend yourself or someone else? to defend your country? What ways of resisting evil without using violence can you think of?

N

YOUR NAME
is the word by which you are known

WHEN A PERSON is brought into the Church of Christ by baptism, he is given his own special name or names: not Anderson or Jones, which identify his family, but James, or Stephen, or Ann. These are examples of what we call Christian names, given when a person is "christened" or made a Christian. The other name used in the service of baptism is the Name of God—"Father, Son, and Holy Ghost." The two names, God's and the person's, are linked together in the covenant by which the Church makes the person a "member of Christ, the child of God." (See "Covenant.")

Your Christian name, therefore, has importance and is generally used in church in special prayers on your birthday, when you are sick, or when you are married.

If our names are important, it is easy to see why God's Name is much more so. If a man uses God's Name in a law court when promising to speak the truth, saying, "So help me God," it means that he calls God to witness to what he says. The third Commandment, "Thou shalt not take the Name of the Lord thy God in vain," includes the reverent use of God's Name.

All truly Christian prayers are prayed in the Name of Jesus Christ, that is, in His Spirit. The idea is that the prayer is the kind of prayer that Jesus would have prayed, asking for things that are according to God's will.

Suggestions for further reading

The Hymnal: 268 (stanzas 1, 2), 323, 325, 326.
Other articles: Baptism, Godparents.

Questions

What did Peter mean when he said, ". . . in the name of Jesus Christ of Nazareth, walk"? (Acts 3:6)

Are you likely to use Jesus' Name properly in your prayers if you use it carelessly at other times? Why are people named for other people? What are some of the different names for God?

O

TO OBEY
means to do what we are told

I MUST DO WHAT I AM TOLD by those who have the right to tell me. Those whom I ought to respect and honor do have this right: my parents, my teachers, my Scout leaders, the coach of my team, the umpire—and above all, God. I usually believe that it is right to obey, even though I may protest. I may not want to turn off the TV and do my homework. But my parents tell me to do it, and I know they have the right to tell me—so I do it.

God wants me to be a certain kind of person. In the Bible and in the life of the Church, He has told me certain things I must do in order to be this kind of person. These things are right because they fit into His plan for His universe.

If we have to choose between obeying God and obeying another person, then we should obey God.

Suggestions for further reading

The Hymnal: 570.
Other articles: Authority, Law, Sin.

Questions

What in us makes it hard to be obedient?

ORDINATION
see Bishop, Deacon, Priest

ORIGINAL SIN
see Fall, Image, Sin

P

A PARABLE

*is a story or description of something familiar intended
to help us to understand something about religion*

A PARABLE IS A COMPARISON. It may be a little story about
human beings which tells us something about God and His
kingdom. It may be a simple description which makes
clear a religious truth.

Parables are not moral fables like those of Aesop and
La Fontaine. Neither are they allegories in which each
detail represents something other than itself. They all tell
of situations which the listeners know about. Each parable
makes just one point.

Jesus used many parables. His parables show what God's
kingdom is like, how much God loves us, and how we
should behave toward other people. Some parables are so
short that they were really pictures-in-words. They concern planting seeds, making bread, lighting a lamp, catching
a fish in a net, finding a lost coin—things that might happen
any day. One is about a boy coming home, another about
a traveler being rescued, another about guests not showing
up for a party.

Jesus was a master at using parables. Here are two examples:

You light a lamp in order to light up a dark room. It would be stupid to cover up the lamp with a pail or a barrel.

God's message is meant to bring joy to people. If you have this joy, it is silly to keep it a secret.

A woman dropped a coin on the floor. When she found it, she was very happy.

God keeps on seeking for the sinner who is lost until He finds him. When He finds him, He rejoices.

By such parables, Jesus is saying that if this is true about something you know, it is much more true about God. Stories, though sometimes very simple, are often the best way to make people think for themselves.

Suggestions for further reading

The Hymnal: 401.
Other articles: Revelation.

THE PASSION OF OUR LORD
was His suffering for us

THE SUFFERING OF JESUS, including all that happened to Him from Palm Sunday through Good Friday, makes up what we call His passion. The six days beginning with Palm Sunday and ending with Good Friday, from His march into Jerusalem to His death on the Cross, are the most solemn part of the Lenten Season.

The word *passion* in this case means "suffering," with the special idea of enduring something which must be borne. Our Lord was willing to endure suffering and death because, as always, He chose to do His Father's will rather than what was easy. As a result He experienced the cruel actions of people who misunderstood and hated Him. It was His obedience that redeemed us, and He could not obey without the suffering and death which that obedience brought on. By His passion, Jesus shows us how far God will go to help His children. Jesus was not seeking death but seeking victory, and He found both.

Suggestions for further reading

The Hymnal: 65, 68, 75, 336, 337.
Other articles: Atonement, Calvary, Cross, Easter, Redemption.

Questions

What difference would it make if Jesus had tried to escape the Cross? What do you understand by the question "Were you there when they crucified my Lord?" (Hymn 80)

PENITENCE
is turning to God in sorrow
after we have done something wrong

THE WORDS *penitence* and *repentance* both concern sorrow for having done something that is wrong. They are not exactly the same. Penitence means "I am very sorry." To be truly sorry I don't have to be all stirred up inside, but I do have to admit my fault and resolve to change my ways. Repentance refers more to the things I do because I am sorry. For instance, I turn to God; I confess my sins; I pray that the injury I have done to another person may be healed; and I determine to help to heal it. I promise myself, and God, that I will try to do better next time.

If you start to smoke, having promised not to, and get caught, you may feel sorry about it. If you are sincere in your feeling, you are penitent. Whether or not you are repentant will depend upon what you do about it. When you admit your mistake and promise that you will not do it again until you are old enough, you are beginning a "turnabout." This action is necessary for penitence to become repentance. You may be sorry that you got caught, but simply try to find a more secret place to smoke the next time. In this case you are neither penitent nor repentant.

If you realize you have hurt your parents, who love you and trust you, this is more like *contrition*. Contrition is the word we use to express our sorrow at offending God. It is the deepest way of being sorry for our sins. There are other ways. In the list that follows pick out the Christian motive for being sorry for some misdeed.

I am sorry for what I did—

1. Because it got me into trouble.
2. Because it made me sick.
3. Because it is against God and He will punish me.
4. Because it made somebody mad at me.
5. Because it is against God and He has been good to me.
6. Because it makes me feel ashamed.

What is the matter with each of the other five?

Here are some psalms of penitence: 32, 51, 130. After reading these penitential psalms, read Psalm 103.

These psalms will help you understand the meaning of penitence. They will also help you to see that once you have acknowledged your sin, God forgives you. You will see that all these psalms end in an act of praise and thanksgiving for forgiveness.

Suggestions for further reading

Other articles: Absolution, Atonement, Confession, Forgiveness, Reconciliation.

Questions

What does the Church do for people who are repentant? How does the Church help us to move from penitence to repentance?

PENTECOST
*is the Jewish feast day on which the Holy Spirit
came to those who believed in the Risen Christ*

PENTECOST WAS THE NAME given to the Jewish festival which occurred fifty days after the Passover. (*Pentecost* means "fiftieth.") The Feast of the Fiftieth Day has several Old Testament names: the Feast of the Harvest (Exod. 23:16), the Feast of Weeks (Deut. 16:10), the Day of the First Fruits (Num. 28:26). But regardless of its name, it was one of the three great agricultural festivals on which all males were required to make a pilgrimage to the Temple at Jerusalem. (Exod. 34:18, 22–23 and II Chron. 8:12–13)

The little band of Jews who were believers in the Risen

Christ were worshiping together in Jerusalem on the Feast of Pentecost following our Lord's resurrection and ascension. Suddenly they knew the Holy Spirit was in their midst. This first Christian Pentecost is described in the second chapter of Acts. We now call this feast day Whitsunday. Read the article on Whitsunday for the Christian significance of this great day.

PRAYER
is close fellowship with God

YOU AND YOUR BEST FRIEND came to know each other well partly through being together and talking together. People get to know each other as they share their thoughts. This is true in our families as well as with our friends.

In much the same way, we get to know God. Being with God and talking with Him is called *prayer*. Prayer begins with God, for He is more interested in listening to us than we are in talking with Him. Through prayer also we find out God's plans for us.

If you want to know someone and want him to know you, you have to be able to say what is on your mind. Some people say it is wrong to pray for material things. But if we want material things, we ought to include them in our prayers. This does not mean that we are asking God to play favorites or to do what He otherwise would not do. It means simply that we are telling Him what is on our minds and leaving the answer to Him. Sometimes as a result of our prayer we may see that we no longer think the things we asked for are important. He may tell us that what we want is all right but that there are other things in life which we ought to want more. If we want God to help us, we have to be honest with Him. This means, first of all, being honest with ourselves.

Prayer to God is of several kinds; here are six, illustrated from the service of Morning Prayer:

1. *Adoration.* Sometimes we are just thankful for God Himself because He is so good, wise, loving, and strong. Adoration is seen in the opening sentence for Trinity Sunday. (Prayer Book, page 5)

2. *Confession.* We admit that we have done wrong or that we have been too lazy or too scared to do right, and we ask God to forgive us. This is what we do in the General Confession. (Page 6)

3. *Meditation.* There are times when we keep still and think, to find out what God wants. The lessons in Morning Prayer provide us with opportunity for meditation. (Pages x–xlv)

4. *Intercession.* We ask God for good things for others, as when we pray for a friend who is sick. When we pray for someone else, we are asking God to bless him, to strengthen our friendship for that person, to help us to understand him more and to be sensitive to what he really needs. One result of praying for someone may be that we think of something which we ourselves ought to do to help that person. The Prayer for all Conditions of Men is an intercession. (Page 18)

5. *Thanksgiving.* We recollect with gratitude the great things God has done for His people. We are thankful for His love and care and for the many good things that have happened to us and to others. The General Thanksgiving is a good example. (Page 19)

6. *Petition.* We ask God for things for ourselves, as

when we say, "Give us this day our daily bread," or when we ask Him to help us do what is right. We see an example of a petition in the Prayer of St. Chrysostom. (Page 20)

Because we are fond of our friends, we seek them out to be with them and talk with them. In that way we get to know them better. In a similar way, by being with God, by listening to Him, and by talking to Him through prayer, we grow to know and love Him better.

Suggestions for further reading

The Hymnal: 405, 419.

Other articles: Absolution, Faith, Fellowship, Holy Communion, Liturgy, Worship.

Questions

How many of these six kinds of prayers are in the Lord's Prayer? How many in Holy Communion? When a boy talks with his father, their relationship deepens; the important thing is that they are in communication with each other. What has this to do with prayer?

A PRIEST
is a minister to whom our Lord gives authority to celebrate Holy Communion and to pronounce the Absolution and Blessing in God's Name

IN THE THREE ORDERS of the ministry, the order of the priesthood stands above that of deacons and below that of bishops. The priest is ordained "to minister to the people committed to his care; to preach the word of God; to baptize; to celebrate the Holy Communion; to pronounce

Absolution and Blessing in God's Name." (Prayer Book, page 294) Only a priest or bishop can perform the last two of these acts. A bishop is first a priest and, of course, loses none of his powers as a priest when he is consecrated bishop.

Usually a priest is the pastor of a congregation given to him as his special care. Only someone who has been ordained priest may be rector of the parish.

To get a clearer idea of the responsibilities of a priest, read the service of ordination in the Prayer Book, pages 536–548. Notice especially the emphasis on the priest as a teacher of his people. (Page 542)

Suggestions for further reading

The Hymnal: 219, 233 (stanzas 1 and 6).

Other articles: Absolution, Bishop, Deacon, Holy Communion, Layman, Minister, Sacrifice.

A PROPHET
is one who speaks as God's messenger

THE GREAT PROPHETS of Old Testament times spoke God's message to the people. They spoke on behalf of God. God used their minds, their imaginations, their skills, their voices. When they felt sure that God was commanding them to speak, they did so whatever their message might be. Although they warned the people of what might happen in the future, their main purpose was to bring God's demand for repentance and reform. To do this, they explained the true meaning of things that were happening at the time—an invasion, a famine, injustice in the courts.

143

They believed that the Spirit of God gave them their thoughts, told them what to say, and filled them with courage and power to say it.

The great words of the prophets taught the people, warned them, and gave them hope. In prosperous times, when there was plenty of wealth, they usually warned the people of God's judgment. To people who were proud, conceited, or selfish, they declared that God did not think big houses and expensive clothes were as important as justice, goodness, and obedience to Him. Sometimes they said that a dreadful punishment was about to fall upon the nation for its sins. In bad times, when most of the people were poor or worried, the prophets assured them that God had not forgotten them but was willing and able to save them. Sometimes the prophets gave glowing word-pictures of a marvelous time when God would rule the entire earth. Some of them told of the coming of a Great Deliverer, God's Messiah, and of the many strange, new, and good things that would happen when He came.

You can read interesting accounts of the prophets in the Old Testament. Some of the prophets are Moses, Isaiah, Jeremiah, Hosea, Amos, and Micah.

Suggestions for further reading

The Hymnal: 19 (stanza 5), 538.
Other articles: Revelation.

Questions

Are there any prophets today?

PROTESTANT
means standing up for something

THE WORD *protestant*, which is often misunderstood, began its religious history in Germany over four hundred years ago. The authorities of the Roman Catholic Church were insisting that the pope and the Church of Rome should continue to have full authority over all Germany. At a great meeting[1] men from certain cities and states stood up and spoke out for their right to religious freedom. Because of the power of the Roman Church, it took courage for a man to stand up for his beliefs and rights and freedoms. These men, many of them princes, were admiringly called "protestants" because they had been brave enough to witness for their belief. (The word *protestant* comes from *pro-test*, *pro*, "for," plus *testari*, "to be a witness.")

The name came to be applied to Lutherans in Germany. Later it spread in usage all over Europe and Great Britain; it came to be used to describe all those who were members of reformed churches and did not give allegiance to the pope.

After the signing of the Declaration of Independence, the Anglicans in America needed a name for their church. They could not very well continue to call themselves members of the Church of England. At a church convention in Maryland, in 1780, the delegates voted to call themselves "The Protestant Episcopal Church." This was more of a description than a name. They were "protestants" because theirs was a form of Christianity not owing allegiance to the pope. They were "episcopal" because the

---

[1] Diet of Spiers, 1529.

office of bishops, or the episcopate, was the most conspicu-
ous feature which distinguished their church from other
non-Roman bodies. The name was not original with them;
it had been used during the colonial period to describe our
church. This time, however, the name stuck as a title and
not just a description. In 1783 the Church in Maryland
made it their official name. Later the whole American
Church adopted it, more by common consent than by
official action.

There are three words which we must think of when
we hear the word *protestant*.

1. *Persons. Protestant* reminds us that witness is a part
of our Christian duty. We are meant to bear witness to our
faith, to stand up for what we believe. To be a child of
God means to be a person, and one is not a person unless
he stands on his own feet.

2. *Truth*. The responsibility to stand up for what one
believes includes the right to doubt and the right to criti-
cize. When we preserve this right, we keep the door open
for a greater knowledge of God's truth. God's truth is too
big to be completely known and understood by any person
or even any group. The Church is the guardian of God's
Word and sacraments, but we have the right to stand up
for a side of the truth which seems to be slighted. Even
the Church can be criticized and can be judged. God can
use men as His agents in judgment as well as in love and
mercy. In trying to explain Christian truth in a day of
questioning and criticism, the Church has developed great
thinkers and discovered new depths of truth. If no one
questions, no one has to explain, and we become lazy
thinkers, or we do not think at all.

3. *Catholic. Protestant* and *catholic* are often thought of

as opposite terms. They should be thought of as companion words, each standing for something the other needs. *Catholic* emphasizes our loyalty to the whole Church and to its long life down through the ages. *Protestant* emphasizes the fact that the Church is not above being criticized and questioned.

Unthinking loyalty turns leaders into bullies and followers into sheep. On the other hand, criticism apart from love and loyalty will undermine and destroy Christian brotherhood. The words *catholic* and *protestant* are like two sides of a coin; each is necessary to the other. We need both to describe the Church.

Suggestions for further reading

Other articles: Catholic, Church, Judgment, Witness.

THE PSALTER
is the Prayer Book name for the Book of Psalms in the Bible

THE PSALTER (pronounced *salter*) is found in the Old Testament between the Book of Job and the Book of Proverbs. It is the only book of the Bible which the Book of Common Prayer contains in full. It occupies 183 of the 600 pages of the Prayer Book. Why is this one book of the Bible given so much room? The answer is that the psalms are wonderfully useful for public worship. They are really hymns and prayers, and they were used as such in the Temple in Jerusalem. They can be either sung or said. They have good rhythm. Many of them are filled with praise. They are about God: His power and beauty, His dealings with us, His rule over all nature. In these great songs He is thought of as Creator, as King, as being filled with mercy and truth. In some of the psalms we appeal to God as our only help in times of national or personal danger and stress. In others we show our thanksgiving and our trust. If you compare one of the psalms in the Book of Common Prayer with the same psalm in your Bible, either the King James translation or the Revised Standard Version, you will find a good many differences. This is because our Prayer Book uses a translation that is older than either.

Suggestions for further reading

The Hymnal: Many of our hymns are based on the Psalms; for example, Hymns 289, 345, 448, and 484. Look for some others.

R

RECONCILIATION
is the act of enabling two people to become friends again

JACK'S FATHER HAD A NECKTIE which a friend had sent him from Scotland. He wore it only on special, dress-up occasions, and then he felt very handsome. Jack thought the tie was good looking, too. One evening when getting dressed to go to the movies with the gang, Jack put on his father's tie. He hadn't asked permission, and he knew that his father really wouldn't want him to wear it. So when he passed the living-room door, he was careful that the tie was covered by his scarf and overcoat collar.

After the movie, the gang went to the soda fountain. There it happened. Jack jokingly flipped a few drops of water on Ned across the table. Quick as a flash the two boys were wrestling, and Ned grabbed the tie and ripped it.

The rest of the evening was no fun for Jack. When he got home, his father was still sitting in the living room, reading. Sooner or later he'd find out, so Jack decided he'd just go in and face the music.

It was hard to do. Father heard him out without changing expression, though when he first saw the torn tie, his lips tightened. Finally, when it was all blurted out, Father motioned Jack to a chair. They talked about why Jack had taken the tie and about how much the tie meant to Father. They both knew they couldn't get another like it. They talked about what would be the right penalty—severe enough, but fair.

And then a wonderful thing happened. Jack felt better, and Father was actually smiling! It was strange, but Jack felt closer to his father now than he had for a long time. They talked about lots of things, things important to both of them. The necktie incident seemed far off, and the feeling of being on good terms, even better than before, was wonderful. Father's understanding of the situation was what did it.

This is an example of human reconciliation.

The Bible says, "God was in Christ reconciling the world to himself." (II Cor. 5:19) Christ came into the world and lived, suffered, and died to bring man, whose sinfulness had kept him apart from God, back into a sound relationship with his heavenly Father. Christ rebuilt our friendship with God; there is new hope for us. What had kept us apart need no longer keep us apart. Only God could have brought about this wonderful change.

Our way of showing our thankfulness for God's reconciling love is to try to be the kind of persons God wants us to be in our relationships with others. He loves *all* of us, not just some of us.

Suggestions for further reading

The Hymnal: 343, 479.

Other articles: Absolution, Atonement, Forgiveness, Incarnation, Redemption, Saviour.

REDEMPTION
is ransoming or rescuing at cost

YOU HAVE JUST COME OUT of a movie and are turning the corner. Suddenly several masked men grab you. Before you can scream, they clap a hand over your mouth. Then they blindfold and gag you, tie your hands, and toss you into a car. You feel the car lurch around the turns, but you soon give up trying to figure out which way you're going. At last the brakes scream, and the kidnapers drag you into their hide-out. Holding a gun to your head, they force you to write a letter asking your parents to pay a hundred thousand dollars and telling them not to breathe a word to the police or you will be killed.

Your parents try and try to raise the money, but they can't—it is far too much. They are almost crazy with grief and fear. Just as they are giving up hope, an old friend comes in and pays your ransom. It takes every penny he has, but he gives it gladly in order to rescue you.

God has "ransomed" us all, but in a very different way. God did not make a deal with any power of evil, yet it is true that ransoming us from our sin caused Him to suffer. Even we, when we forgive someone, have to suffer; forgiving a person *means* "taking it" when he hurts us and forgiving him in spite of it. God the Son "took" all the sins of all mankind and, by suffering as man, brought about men's forgiveness. It cost Him His life to do this. Because what He did to rescue us was so costly, we call it *ransoming* or *redemption*.

We have to accept our redemption. We are our own captors; it is our own bad habits that hold us slaves. Yet we cannot free ourselves. We are like lassoed steers: the harder we pull, the tighter goes the rope. Only God can set us free. But even He can free us only when we ourselves are willing to let Him.

We must let Him free us in His own way. We must let Him take us into the fellowship of His Church, and in that fellowship we must accept each other as we are. Our fellow Christians are not saints, but neither are we. God accepts us, so we accept them.

If we accept them generously, God can use us, not to redeem others—only God can redeem—but to help them go free. He has already "paid" for our freedom. But He lets us help to untie others, and as we do this, He unties us, too.

Suggestions for further reading

The Hymnal: 65.

Other articles: Absolution, Atonement, Communion of Saints, Forgiveness, Mediator, Reconciliation, Sacrament, Sin.

Questions

How would you say in your own words what Jesus said to James and John in St. Mark 10:42–45? When a bad man straightens out, we often say he has redeemed himself. What *should* we say? Why do we often call the Christian fellowship "redemptive"?

REJECTION
is the act of leaving someone out

HAVE YOU EVER FELT that no one liked you or wanted to have you around? Maybe you weren't chosen for a spelling match. Maybe a teacher was too busy to notice you when you came back to school after being sick a week. Maybe three or four friends knew a joke and didn't tell you. Maybe someone hurried down the street instead of waiting for you. Left out, you were rejected.

When this happens to us, we begin to dislike other people. Sometimes we don't even like ourselves. We aren't always sure what is wrong, but whatever it is makes us act in a disagreeable way. We may sulk, or be rude, or pretend to be extra important by showing off or boasting. The things we say very loudly are meant to make us more sure of ourselves. We have to feel important to make up for all the doubts that come when we suspect we have been rejected. Sometimes we pretend we really don't want any friends and can get along nicely alone. We may even refuse to go somewhere we want to go, just to prove we don't care about other people.

But there is a better way of living with rejection. Jesus Christ knew all there was to know about rejection. He prayed for those who were nailing Him to the cross. Whatever happens to us, we know He understands. He is with us to support and strengthen us.

Some day, with His help, we may come to see that the experience of being rejected was good for us even if it hurt. If we were accepted always, we might be too satisfied with ourselves! We may need to be taken down a bit once in a while so that we will change and grow and understand.

Experience in being rejected is especially valuable in showing us how other people feel and in helping us to reach out to them. Try to remember what has happened when a boy or girl is disagreeable. He or she really needs help to be at ease again. The situation would become worse for everyone if we rejected him further because of the way he showed his feelings. It doesn't matter whose fault it is. The real need is to heal the hurt.

Perhaps a person thinks that his friends have rejected him when they haven't at all. It's just a misunderstanding or something the person imagines. But the hurt feeling is just as bad as if the rejection were real.

The opposite of rejection is acceptance. If we understand rejection, we understand acceptance. And the clue to the whole thing is that we can accept others because God accepts us. Even when we are most obnoxious, He accepts us and loves us.

Suggestions for further reading

The Hymnal: 407.
Other articles: Acceptance, Heaven, Hell, Separation.

Questions

What can we do in our own group when we have been rejected? What kind of people are we most likely to reject: Those of a different religion? A different race? Those with no money? Those who are unpopular? Those who are different and don't follow the crowd?

What can we do for one who has been rejected?

RELIGION
is the way I live and think and act in giving loyalty to God

IF YOU WERE ASKED SUDDENLY, "What is religion," and you had no time to think about it, what would you say?

Maybe something like this: "It's that business about Church, and—or—God, and being good, and all that."

For a quick answer that would not be bad. Religion is what receives one's loyalty and makes life worth living, or it is what one obeys. But to say *only* that would leave God out of the picture. And God is the *object* of our religion.

Now lots of people have religions that are built around false or partial pictures of God. Of course there is only one real God. But if you let something else be the supreme thing in your life, then we can say that it is your "god," because you have put it in the place of the real God. If money is all that matters to a person, that means he has made money his "god." Or if someone makes fun the most important thing in his life, then fun is his "god." People sometimes go all out for power, or for fame, or for something else. If they let any of these "gods" take over, they are worshiping an idol, a false god. Our religion is not just something we thought up for ourselves or chose because we liked it. It is our way of responding in thought, word, and deed to *what God is* and to *what God has done*. This is why religion was defined in the title of this article as the way we live and think and act in loyalty to God. We live in gratitude for what He has done for us.

There are nine great religions in the world today. Of these, two started in India, Hinduism and Buddhism; two began in China, Confucianism and Taoism; one in Japan, Shintoism; one in Persia, Zoroastrianism. Two started in Arabia, Judaism and Mohammedanism. The birthplace of Christianity was Palestine. Of all these religions, the one with the greatest number of followers is Christianity, with more than five hundred million members. Next in order

155

come Confucianism, Hinduism, and Mohammedanism, with around two hundred and forty million each.

Only Judaism and Mohammedanism are like Christianity in pointing us to a God who is personal, who wants personal companionship with us, and who is also the supreme being who controls the whole universe. Christianity is the *only* religion that has a Gospel, a chronological story about the redemption of man by God, offered freely as a gift, not earned.

Here are some definitions of religion:

1. A belief in a Supreme Power outside yourself, to whom you feel a sense of obligation, including obedience, and whose influence upon your life brings a joyous feeling

2. Your life lived in the knowledge of God, whom you trust, with whom you have companionship, whom you worship and try to obey.

3. The life of God in the soul of man.

4. Life lived as in the presence of God.

Nobody who practices a certain religion will be satisfied with any one of these definitions because he will want to add certain things. Christians always make Jesus Christ the center of the definition of their religion.

Suggestions for further reading

The Hymnal: 258, 493, 498.
Other articles: Christian, God, Incarnation, Trinity.

REPENTANCE
see Penitence

RESURRECTION
means rising after death

To READ ABOUT our Lord's resurrection, see the article on Easter. St. Paul tells about it in this way: "For I delivered to you as of first importance what I also received, that Christ died for our sins in accordance with the scriptures, that he was buried, that he was raised on the third day in accordance with the scriptures, and that he appeared to Cephas, then to the twelve. Then he appeared to more than five hundred brethren at one time, most of whom are still alive, though some have fallen asleep. Then he appeared to James, then to all the apostles. Last of all, as to one untimely born, he appeared also to me." (I Cor. 15:3–8) This is our faith, too.

Christians are not only witnesses to the resurrection of Jesus Christ but have the hope of resurrection for themselves. For Jesus Christ is not only truly a man, but also representative of all humanity. He has made it possible for us to be caught up in His risen life. He draws us upward with Himself to eternal life with God. That is why the Creed speaks of "The Resurrection of the body: And the Life everlasting."

We believe that when we are redeemed and raised from the dead, we shall be raised as whole and complete persons. God provided us with a body so we could live in this world. We are confident that He will provide us with a body which will be suitable for our life in the world to come.

As one of the closing prayers of the baptismal service puts it: ". . . grant, that he [who has just been baptized], being dead unto sin, may live unto righteousness, and being buried with Christ in his death, may also be partaker of his resurrection; so that finally, with the residue of thy holy Church, he may be an inheritor of thine everlasting kingdom . . ."

Suggestions for further reading

The Hymnal: 587.
Other articles: Easter, Inheritor, Kingdom of God, Soul and Spirit.

Questions

What are the important things for most people in the celebration of Easter? Why do many people want to make their communion on Easter?

REVELATION
is God's making Himself known to man

THE BIBLE IS THE RECORD of how God disclosed Himself to people through many years. He did this gradually, not all at once, which we can understand if we think of getting to know people in our own lives. For instance, you might write to someone your own age in England. After a while, because of the letters, that person would seem less like a stranger and more like a friend. Then suppose he visits this country, and you receive a telephone call from him. How much more you would know about him now. His tone of voice reveals the real person better than words on paper could. Finally, he comes to see you. Then you really get acquainted.

So it was that God revealed Himself to people over a

number of centuries. The Bible shows God acting in history. He created everything. He freed the Israelites from slavery in Egypt. By this act He made Himself known to Israel. (Read Psalm 105.) He later showed Himself through the words of the prophets, who were His spokesmen. Finally He *came* to us in the person of Jesus Christ. This means that God the Son came to us in human life as a real man named Jesus. "And the Word became flesh and dwelt among us . . ." (John 1:14) God revealed Himself supremely in Christ's person, His work, His life, death, resurrection, ascension, and the promise of His coming again. This was the high point of God's personal communication to us.

Suggestions for further reading

The Hymnal: 402.
Other articles: God, Holy Spirit, Incarnation.

Questions

Does God still reveal Himself to us? What acts of God are most important to you?

RIGHT
is that which is in accord with God's purpose

THERE IS USUALLY A RIGHT WAY to do things and a wrong way to do them. There are right reasons for doing things and wrong reasons for doing them. How do we know what is right?

We know by the way things are meant to work. Boys know that there is a proper way to use a crosscut saw. If the saw isn't used in this way, it doesn't work very well, and the wood may splinter. Girls know that there is a correct way to knit; if it isn't followed the yarn snarls. We know that it is better for people to get along with each other than to quarrel. If people are going to get along, they have to be willing to listen to each other. No one person's word is the law unless everybody agrees to it. If people are going to get along together, they have to be considerate of each other. They must also be reliable and carry out what they say they will do.

We also learn about right from the experiences of other people. Is it necessary for every boy or girl to be hit by a truck in order to learn to ride a bicycle safely? We can learn about right and wrong from observing the results of other people's actions as well as our own.

Our laws try to set forth what is right to keep people from hurting themselves and each other. It is right to drive within the speed limit because experience has shown that exceeding the speed limit is unsafe. It is wrong to drive carelessly because it violates Christ's law of love and concern for others. It is right to use the police and the courts to get certain problems straightened out because we know that there will be more justice this way. It is wrong to take the law in our own hands, trying to impose punishment ourselves, because this would make us savages. It is right to pay our taxes because we pay for our government through them. It is wrong to avoid paying our own way because we must share responsibility.

God's law is that anything which relates us to God's purpose is right and anything which interferes with God's purpose is wrong. The Bible and the Book of Common Prayer help us to understand God's plan for our lives and therefore help us to understand right and wrong.

Suggestions for further reading

The Hymnal: 11, 447, 563, 570.

Other articles: Conscience, Good, Kingdom of God, Law, Murder.

THE ROGATION DAYS
are the three days before Ascension Day

ASCENSION DAY OR HOLY THURSDAY is forty days after Easter (counting Easter as the first day). The Monday, Tuesday, and Wednesday in the same week are the Rogation Days. The Sunday just before them is called Rogation Sunday. *Rogation* means "asking," and on these three days we ask God to bless the earth and make it fruitful so that there will be enough food for all of us. It is natural to ask this in the spring when seeds are beginning to sprout. We want good crops, and we know that it is by God's goodness that we have them. In the autumn at Thanksgiving time, we thank God for what we have received.

Following an ancient custom, the Rogation Day prayers are often said out-of-doors. Usually led by a minister and perhaps a choir, the people march in a procession around the fields and through the gardens to bless the crops.

Suggestions for further reading

The Hymnal: 101, 138.

Questions

How can a city church observe Rogation Sunday?

S

SABBATH
see Sunday

A SACRAMENT
is an outward sign by which God gives us grace

A FAMILY THAT DOES THINGS TOGETHER has fun. The happiest families are the ones that play together, eat together, hike and climb and swim together, garden together, sing together. The things they do together make for family love and joy.

In God's family the big things we do together are the *sacraments*—sacred acts of God's Church. God gives His gift of power through an outward sign so that we can all act with Him. It is outward so that every member of the Family can take part.

In Holy Baptism, for instance, we and God act together. We do not all crowd around the font with pitchers of water to pour on the baby. You can see why not! We let one person pour the water and say the words. (Prayer Book, page 279) But when he does this he is acting *for us all*. (That is why we call him a "minister," an agent.) It is really *we* who adopt that baby into God's family—we and God.

In Holy Communion we meet at the Family Table. One person, a bishop or a priest, takes the bread and wine and gives thanks. But all through the prayers he says "we," because he is acting for us all—for us and for our Lord. (Prayer Book, pages 80–81) Through the bread and wine that we have asked God to bless, Jesus Himself comes to us and lifts us up together to worship the Father.

These two sacraments are "generally necessary to salvation." That is, we must all receive them if we possibly can. But our Book of Common Prayer gives us five other rites that are so much like sacraments (outward signs bringing inward grace) that many people call them that. Whatever we call them, they too are acts of God's family: we and God do them together. In Confirmation we bring a child of God to receive the Holy Ghost for the work of a grown-up in the Family. (Prayer Book, pages 296–299) In Matrimony we witness the promises and bless the bride and groom. (Prayer Book, pages 300–304) In Penance we let one person, the priest, tell the sinner he is forgiven, but he says this for God and for us all. (Prayer Book, pages 313–314) In Unction we anoint a sick person with oil and pray that God will heal him. (Prayer Book, p. 320) In Orders we give men power and authority to act for God as fathers in His family. (Prayer Book, pages 529–562)

These rites are outward so that we can all act together. Almost all human acts *are* outward. We express ourselves, bring *out* what we mean, by using our lips, our faces, our hands. That is the way human beings are. God the Son became human and still is human. So it is natural that He blesses us the human way—by using outward signs. It is natural, too, that He uses human agents to bless us and a human fellowship to draw us out of ourselves.

Suggestions for further reading

Other articles: Absolution, Baptism, Confirmation, Grace, Holy Communion, Incarnation, Holy Matrimony, Unction of the Sick.

Questions

When two friends make up a quarrel, what is the outward sign? What is the outward sign of an important promise? When does a boy or girl become a Scout? At what moment is a man *in* the Army?

A SACRIFICE
is something valuable to us which we give to God or to other people

YOU DON'T MIND picking up a loaf of bread for your mother if you are going to pass the store on your way home anyway. But if you have to go six blocks out of the way and you want to play football or go to the movies, you are making at least a small sacrifice. A baseball player makes a sacrifice hit when he bunts and is thrown out at first base so that another man can get to second.

If you get your offering from your parents before going to church, your putting it in the plate is no sacrifice for you. If you save it from your allowance or from what you have earned, and offer it in church, it has become a gift or sacrifice.

When we talk about those who have died defending our country, we say they made the "supreme sacrifice."

"Greater love has no man than this, that a man lay down his life for his friends." (John, 15:13) When Jesus died, He was offering Himself for all men.

Many primitive people feel that it is right to set aside some of their food for God. The ancient Hebrews used to pour the blood of animals on the ground and burn food as their sacrifice to Yahweh. They sometimes shared with God in eating the food of the sacrifice as a common meal.

In earliest times, the father in the Hebrew family made the offering to thank God for His blessings. Later on, the priests took over this sacrifice for the tribe or for the community. These sacrifices were replaced by a central sacrifice for the whole nation in the Temple in Jerusalem. Sacrifices became not only signs of thanks, but also a means of seeking forgiveness for sins.

Our sacrifices can never bring us to God. Jesus' sacrifice did that. And when we who belong to the Church *now* act sacrificially in any way at all, we are really making a thank-offering to Him because He died for us. We can do this only through His strength.

When you go to the Holy Communion, you join your little acts of sacrifice with His great act of sacrifice on the Cross. The bread and the wine which we offer in the Holy Communion stand for our little sacrifices. Christ takes them—and takes us, too: "our souls and bodies," our work and our play, and everything else that we offer to him—and He includes them in His own offering to the Father. Then they are blessed in the great thanksgiving for the mighty act of God in Christ. And after we have received Christ's life and strength in the Communion, we go out in gratitude to make more loving acts of self-sacrifice in our daily lives.

Suggestions for further reading

Suggestions for further reading

The Hymnal: 189 (stanza 1), 190, 437.

Other articles: Atonement, Calvary, Holy Communion, Redemption.

Questions

What sacrifices do we make for our families? What do members of our families sacrifice for us? How do we bring our sacrifice to God in the Holy Communion?

A SAINT
is a person who has let God make him holy

GOD WANTS YOU TO BE a saint, not just a fairly decent Christian. You wouldn't eat a "pretty good" egg. You wouldn't fly with a "fair to middling" pilot. Neither does God want you to be second-rate. He will take you—over and over again—the way you are. But He will never stop wanting you to be 100 per cent holy and helping you to be a saint.

Real saints are full of fun. Paul and Silas were thrown into a foul dungeon, their feet in the stocks, their backs throbbing from a beating, and in the middle of the night they began to sing! Lawrence, bound to a gridiron and roasted over a fire, called out to the judge, "Turn me now, I'm done on that side!" We have a saying: "A saint that is sad is a sad saint."

Because saints are joyous, people like them. They crowded around Francis almost as much as they crowded around our Lord. Even animals loved him. Have you read the story of how he tamed the wolf?

All sorts of people became saints. Andrew was a fisherman. Crispin and Crispinian made shoes. Maurice and Sebastian were soldiers, Helena a queen. The Innocents were babies, John a very old man. Joseph was a carpenter, Luke a doctor. The martyrs of Uganda were boys, Agnes and Lucy girls, Thomas a learned scholar, Juniper a fool. There's room for us all!

Many saints have been heroically brave. The heathen agreed to chop down their sacred oak tree if Martin would let them tie him where the tree was sure to fall. "O.K.," said Martin, "tie me." The tree just missed him.

But the saints were not heroes all their lives. When they started they were just like you and me. James and John had fiery tempers. Peter cursed and swore. Matthew bled the people for money. Peter disowned Jesus three times. Yet Jesus made them into saints. He can also do it with us.

How do we start? By letting our Lord love us and forgive us. If we sin again, we must let Him forgive us again, even if He has to do it a million times. For the joy of being forgiven is our first taste of heaven.

Suggestions for further reading

The Hymnal: 243.

Other articles: Communion of Saints, Forgiveness, Heaven, Holy Spirit, Sanctify.

SALVATION
see Atonement, Redemption, Saviour

SANCTIFY
means to make holy

ONLY THE HOLY SPIRIT can make us holy. God does not force Himself upon us, however. We are free to refuse the influence of the Holy Spirit. God begins the work of making us holy, but we must be willing to have it happen. We must let the Holy Spirit work within us to help us. Through Him we become mature men and women, measured with Christ as a standard. (See Ephesians 4:11–16.)

Not only do we pray that the Holy Spirit will sanctify our lives, but we ask that He put power into those things which are used for sacred purposes in our worship. We ask God to sanctify the water used for baptism, the bread and wine in Holy Communion, and to "direct, sanctify, and govern, both our hearts and bodies."

The Holy Spirit works to sanctify us through the Church's sacraments, through other people, through Christian groups to which we belong. He always works to bring our plans and actions into agreement with God's holy will.

Suggestions for further reading

The Hymnal: 256, 463.
The Book of Common Prayer: 70, 81, 279.
Other articles: Grace, Hallow, Holy Spirit, Saint.

Questions

How would you answer a friend who said, "If I try to be holy, I can't go to parties and have fun"?

OUR SAVIOUR
is Jesus Christ who saves us from sin

IF YOU WERE SWIMMING beyond your depth and began to sink, your rescuer would have to know how to swim, be more skillful than you, and be willing to help you at whatever cost to himself.

Our Saviour Jesus Christ understands the situation we are in. He was human and was tested as we are tested. No one of us can go through a test so hard that Jesus does not understand. He was the only one who ever won a complete victory over temptations. His whole human life was marked by complete obedience to the Father, leaving no room for selfish desires.

We say in the Nicene Creed that He who is "God of God, Light of Light, Very God of very God; Begotten, not made; Being of one substance with the Father, . . . for us men and for our salvation came down from heaven. . . ." That is, He came to save us and to give us the whole and healthy lives we need. By His complete obedience, even to His death on the Cross, He makes it possible for us to be saved. The name Jesus means "the Lord will save."

A person struggling in deep water is saved *from* drowning and *for* continued life. In every case of saving there is a *from* and a *for*. Jesus Christ saves us *from* the dreadful lostness, the separation to which our sins would otherwise condemn us, and saves us *for* a new life of trust in God and fellowship in Christ's Church.

Suggestions for further reading

The Hymnal: 272, 349.

Other articles: Atonement, Incarnation, Mediator, Redemption, Sanctify.

Questions

If someone gets into juvenile court, how can he be saved *from* jail? How do people work to save him? *For* what is he saved? How would you apply these answers to what Jesus did?

THE SECOND COMING OF OUR LORD
means His coming to judge the living and the dead

THE BOOK OF COMMON PRAYER speaks of the second coming of Christ. The Te Deum (page 10) says, "We believe that thou shalt come to be our Judge." There are similar references in the Creeds and some of the collects.

To get the meaning of this we have to remind ourselves that the whole long history of human beings on this earth is a story not yet finished. Just as it had a beginning, it will also have an end. God is the Author of this story and Chief Actor in it. When He made men and gave them the earth for their home, He had a plan—a purpose. Until now, His plan has not been fully carried out. It is an unfinished story. But when His plan is complete, the end will come. One of the truths about God (true for Him and for no other being) is that *all* His purposes are finally completed. He is never defeated. In the Creed we say Christ will come again with glory. Though He is God and He will judge us justly, He is still man and will judge us with love.

There is a lot of mystery in all this. Just when did the story begin? Just when will it end? Jesus said, "It is not for you to know times or seasons which the Father has fixed by his own authority." (Acts 1:7) We do know that God's purpose is always good and right and that in the end it will triumph, in spite of man's cruelty and greed.

Suggestions for further reading

The Hymnal: 5, 11, 312, 522.

Other articles: Advent, Ascension, Judgment, Kingdom of God.

Questions

How does the atom bomb affect our thinking about the end of the world? Will God's creation run down?

How would you prepare to be judged by someone you love and who loves you?

What help do the prayers on pages 90 and 93 of the Prayer Book give us in understanding the Second Coming?

TO BE SECURE
is to know that one can count on God
even when things go wrong

SOME PEOPLE "play it safe" all the time. They never dare speak up about the things in which they believe for fear someone will laugh at them. They never dare to make a friendly gesture toward the new boy or girl down the street for fear the gang won't agree. They are afraid to compete because they are afraid they may be beaten.

Other people have more fun because they dare to do the things that, deep inside, they know are right for them. They have found out that even if they goof and even if people laugh at them, they are still worthwhile people. Nothing can take from us our place in God's kingdom. We are children of God always.

Suppose you have set your heart on winning a game or a prize, and you lose. You'll be disappointed for a while. But some friend, or maybe an older person, will understand, and you will feel better being with him until you have had a chance to recover. In the same way, a Christian knows that no matter what dangers and fears and disappointments he has in life, he can always be secure in his relationship to God. He is able to count on God, who loves and upholds him. This is also what the psalmist meant: "the LORD is the strength of my life; of whom then shall I be afraid?" (Psalm 27, Prayer Book, page 371)

Suggestions for further reading

The Hymnal: 363, 422, 431.

Other articles: Acceptance, Rejection, Saviour, Separation.

Questions

Some people say, "If you don't try, you can't lose." Others say, "If you don't try, you can't win." What do you think?

SEPARATION

is the broken relationship which results from having unfriendly thoughts or opposing aims

WE USUALLY THINK OF SEPARATION in terms of distance. If your best friend goes away to camp and you stay at home, you are separated for a few weeks. But the word has another meaning, too. Imagine two people who are interested in very different things. One thinks of nothing but athletics and dreams about being a hero in a baseball game or becoming a famous tennis player. The other loves music and is willing to spend hours practicing the violin. The chances are that these two, even if they live in the same town and go to the same school, will be separated from each other because their interests are different.

Now imagine two people, people who have been good friends and have the same interests, having a sudden disagreement. Each sees only his point of view. They quarrel and then do not speak to each other. They have become separated. The friendship seems to be broken, and both are unhappy. Perhaps each continues to think it was all the fault of the other. Neither sees how he could have avoided the disaster.

One kind of separation has to do with distance. The other has to do with ideas and interests that keep people apart. But we see that the most serious kind of separation comes from refusing to see another's viewpoint or to take your share of the blame.

To be separated like this from people around us, from members of our family or from the boys and girls at school, is a bad thing. Usually we "cut ourselves off" from them because they don't do exactly what we want them to do. This "cutting off" does harm on both sides. The smallest package in the world is a person wrapped up in himself!

All of us are at times separated from God in this last way. It happens when we think *we* know best and that God doesn't matter very much. Perhaps we try to tell ourselves that the lie we told yesterday didn't matter; it was only a little lie, and nobody found out. This means that what God wants us to do and to be is not important to us, and so we try to forget Him.

Unlike the case of the two friends who were both to blame for becoming separated, the cause of our separation from God is always in us. He has not sent us into isolation. We have slammed the door and shut ourselves out of His presence.

He still loves us and wants us. He keeps on knocking at the door of our hearts. He will not force His way in, but, whenever we let Him in, He will come in gladly. He will stay out only if we lock Him out. To lock Him out forever would be hell. To let Him back in, and accept His forgiveness, is the beginning of heaven.

Suggestions for further reading

The Hymnal: 211.

Other articles: Confession, Forgiveness, Heaven, Hell, Penitence, Reconciliation, Rejection.

Questions

Consider times when you have felt separated from someone. Was it because of distance, different interests, or disagreements? How was it possible to remedy the separation?

SIN
is separation from God and disobedience to His will

SIN IS A WORD that many people greatly misunderstand. A look at the Book of Common Prayer will help you see that its meaning is really clear. At Morning Prayer we say in the General Confession, "We have left undone those things which we ought to have done; And we have done those things which we ought not to have done; And there is no health in us." The meaning of sin is all packed into that sentence. First, "We have left undone those things which we ought to have done." Our Christian life is not just abstaining from doing bad things; it is also, and more importantly, trying in every way to do good things. But often we deliberately avoid a plain duty; we think of a kind act we ought to do and then just don't do it. That is sin.

Secondly, "we have done those things which we ought not to have done." God has shown us His holy will. In the Ten Commandments and in Jesus' Summary of the Law, we hear and can know our duty. In the life of our Lord Himself, we see the standard which everybody should use to measure his life. But by our own willful choice, we have decided to do what we please. We set up "the kingdom of me" in place of the kingdom of God, and we let our lives be ruled by "me," not God. So we act proudly, claiming to run the show; we act selfishly, preferring our own ideas to God's.

So far we have spoken of *doing*. But in the General Confession in Holy Communion, we say that we have sinned "by thought, word, and deed." We sin just as much in our thinking, in our attitudes, and in our motives as we do in our actions. In our words, too, we can sin badly; for we can say things that hurt, or not say things that help, or fail to say things as God would have us say them, with kindness and regard for the other fellow's feelings. These are called sins of omission (things left out).

But there is a difference between *sins* and *sin*. Sins are the things we do or fail to do. Sin is the condition inside us that makes us do them or fail to do them. It is like an infection in our blood that doesn't show all the time but comes out here and there in ugly boils. Behind all our sinful acts is this inner infecting sin. So it is called *original* sin, because it is the beginning of them all and we all suffer from it.

This original sin separates us from God. Of course in one sense nobody could ever be separated from God. He made us, He keeps us alive, He is always present with us. But while *He* is with us, *we* can be away from Him. We can put ourselves in such a position that it is just as if He weren't there. When we quarrel with a friend, we may be in the same room with him, but we are still separated from him in a very real sense. Thus we say, "there is no health in us," for away from God we are unhealthy. The actual sins that we commit are really ways in which we express this kind of terrible separation we have established between God and ourselves. And we can't get out of this fix by ourselves.

Look up the article, "Fall," and you will see how the Church has talked about all this. But remember that the whole point of the Christian Gospel is that what *we* couldn't do, God has done. *He* has brought us back to be *at one* with him. *He* forgives us our sins. *He* accepts us and restores us. That is why we say in the General Confession in Holy Communion, "For thy Son our Lord Jesus Christ's sake, Forgive us all that is past; And grant that we may ever hereafter Serve and please thee In newness of life, To the honour and glory of thy Name."

Suggestions for further reading

The Hymnal: 404, 410.

Other articles: Conscience, Fall, Judgment, Kingdom of God, Second Coming, Temptation, Trespass.

Questions

When you don't know whether something is a sin or not, what test can you use? What is the reason that the Church uses the word *health* to mean "salvation" in many of its prayers and hymns? Why do we say there is no health *in us*, but that *God* makes us healthy? Why does "left undone" come first in the General Confession?

SOUL AND SPIRIT
are those parts of us that make us fully human

SOUL AND SPIRIT are not parts of us that can be taken out in the way you can take a carburetor out of a car or a nut out of a shell. Body, soul, and spirit are all living parts of us and cannot be divided. Spirit is the "part" that makes each of us different from anyone else in the world. Soul is the "part" that makes us human.

Human beings are animals of a special kind, and it is the soul that makes them special. The soul does not live without a body, but by God's gift of resurrection it may live again in a *new* kind of body.

The spirit is not separate from body and soul. It is more like whatever we mean by *personality*. Other people know our spirits by the way we use our bodies to make ourselves known. Spirit can never be seen by itself, yet you can tell what kind of spirit a man has by the way he does things, by what he is interested in, by how he treats other people, and, especially, by how he acts toward God. A man's spirit is what determines the kind of person he is.

The spirit is shaped and strengthened by worship and by service for others done in Christ's Name. The Holy Spirit of God acts through our spirits. With our spirits we relate to other people. When we pray for others and worship together in church, we are opening up contact between ourselves and other spirits, human and divine. This process is mysterious because we cannot see it happening. It is as real in its results as electrical impulses or radio waves. We cannot see them either, but we know they are at work because they make light, supply power, and give us sounds and TV pictures. Our bodies remind us we are part of the animal world. Our soul-life makes us human. Our spirits are our contact with God and other people.

We speak of these parts as separate things, but God does not deal with "parts." When body, soul, and spirit work properly together, we are "whole" or "saved." When the priest gives us the consecrated Bread and Wine he says that they are to "preserve thy *body* and *soul* unto *everlasting* life." We cannot illustrate this oneness of body, soul, and spirit because there is nothing in the world quite like a human being. That is why people must be treated with such care. The work Jesus did on earth and still does through His Spirit is to make men and women *full* and *real* people in whom spirit, soul, and body are all united in one living person.

Suggestions for further reading

The Hymnal: 154, 375, 376.
Other articles: Heaven, Image, Resurrection.

Questions

Would your body go to climb a mountain if your spirit was not willing? If your spirit wanted to go, could it make your body go on the climb?

TO STEAL
is to take without permission
what belongs to somebody else

STEALING CAN BE taking such a little thing as a postage stamp, or keeping a nickel of extra change, or going to a movie at half price if one ought to pay full price. Cheating on tests in school is really stealing, too. Taking away someone's reputation, or making too many demands on his time, can also be stealing.

If everybody grabbed anything he could, no matter who owned it, there wouldn't be any peace or order among us and no real civilization. Everybody would have to carry a weapon to protect himself. But even worse, there would be no real respect of one person for another. There would be no such thing as generosity or kindness or rejoicing in another's happiness. It would be every man for himself. Force and a sort of sly cleverness would be the rule. It would be a sorry world with no sharing, no self-respect, no honor, no love, no trust.

God wants His people to love and trust and care for one another and to respect each other's belongings. Therefore one of God's commandments is "Thou shalt not steal." The Prayer Book tells us this means "To be true and just in all . . . dealings." (Page 289) So we should beware of stealing another person's work, of taking away his reputation, or of wasting his time.

Suggestions for further reading

Other articles: Adultery, Conscience, False Witness, Sin.

Questions

You may want to discuss cases you know of where stealing seemed to be involved. Was it really stealing? How did it get started? What was the outcome? What would you have done?

Under what circumstances can you be said to steal another person's time by using the telephone?

A STEWARD
is one who has charge of something for someone else

A LONG TIME AGO, the word *steward* meant "ward of the sty" (sty-ward), that is, the keeper of pigs. He was a servant who was responsible for a small portion of his master's property. Today, it means anyone who is responsible for the use of the abilities and possessions God has given him.

Jesus told a parable about a man who, before taking a trip, called three of his servants (stewards) and gave each a sum of money. To the first one he gave five "talents," or about $5,000. in our money. He gave two "talents" to the second man and one to the third. When the master returned, each steward had to report on what he had done with the money entrusted to him. Each had received a different amount, but each was held responsible for putting to use and increasing what he had received. Read the parable for yourself in St. Matthew 25:14–30.

In this parable Jesus wasn't talking about money only. He was talking about abilities as well, and it was from this parable that the word *talent* got its modern meaning. God has given us different talents, some more than others. We cannot take credit for having abilities, but we are held responsible for the way we use them. We may be able to sing or paint or write poetry or run a store or bank. Some of us get better grades than others, some are more popular, some are prettier or more handsome, some are better athletes. We must use our God-given talents and improve them if possible.

In the same way, we are stewards or caretakers of our wealth and possessions. God made it possible for us to possess things. We use them for a while; and when we die, others will use them. I may talk about "my" money. It is not mine; it is God's! Some of us have bigger homes and more spending money than others. One family has a larger car than another. But whatever wealth and possessions we have are really God's, given to us for a time to use for Him.

I am meant to be a good steward of God's wealth, using it wisely so that it will bring happiness to others and glory to God.

Suggestions for further reading

The Hymnal: 481, 500 (stanza 2), 732, 733.
Other articles: Faith, Obey, Sacrifice, Witness.

Questions

If you don't take care of the band instrument you play because it belongs to the school, not to you, what does this imply?

SUNDAY

is the Lord's day, for worship and rest

THE KEEPING OF ONE DAY of the week as a non-working day is very ancient and has long been a custom among primitive tribes of all sorts as well as among Jews, Christians, and Moslems. The story of the Creation in Genesis tells us that even God rested after He made the world. That is why Jews observe the seventh day of the week, as the Fourth Commandment clearly explains. The Jews think of Saturday, or the Sabbath as they call it, as a time to rest from everyday work, indoors and out, and also as a special holy day on which to remember the partnership between God and His people. It is a day for rejoicing in the Lord.

Christians, however, had a new reason for rejoicing: Christ had risen from the dead. This changed not only their lives but also their calendars. It was on Sunday, the first day of the week, that women came to the tomb and learned that Jesus had risen from the dead. This was the wonderful new event by means of which God, in Jesus Christ, showed Himself victor over sin and death. They celebrated the day of Resurrection every week as well as every year.

At first Christians observed both the seventh day and the first day of each week. Gradually, however, the observance of the Sabbath dropped out of Christian observance as the keeping of the Lord's Day became more and more important. Each Sunday was a little Easter, and we still celebrate it as such: "O God, who makest us glad with the weekly remembrance of the glorious resurrection of thy Son, our Lord. . . ." (Prayer Book, page 595) For a long time the Greek name for Sunday was "the Day of Resurrection." Our Quaker friends still call it "First Day."

Our Sunday is a day of joy and worship, and it also provides a time for rest, a change of schedule, and family recreation. Although bus operators, service-station attendants, waiters in restaurants, policemen, firemen, and many others have to work on Sunday, factories, banks, and most stores are closed, and so are schools.

By setting aside one day particularly for churchgoing, rest, and recreation, we remind ourselves that life has a meaning not seen on the surface and that God stands at the center of our daily decisions. We may also get new physical and spiritual energy to perform our work better.

Suggestions for further reading

The Hymnal: 96.
Other articles: Easter, Resurrection, Worship.
The Bible: Revelation 1:10.

Questions

Compare the way the Puritans wanted Sunday to be observed and the way it is observed today. What does "keep holy the Sabbath Day" mean to you? Why do some people object to movies on Sunday?

A CHRISTIAN SYMBOL

is a sign or object which stands for an important fact about God and brings it home to us

IF YOU SAW A PICTURE of a cut-down cherry tree and a hatchet and were asked what it stood for, you would say,

"For George Washington when he was a boy." This is a symbol, because there is no picture of young George in it. It is the fallen tree and hatchet that bring the story to your mind. The highway sign showing a child running is a caution that there are children in the neighborhood; drive carefully, it says. Symbols are useful. If you know what they mean, you can "read" them in less time than it takes to read the words that would have to be used in their place.

For centuries people have agreed that crossed keys stand for St. Peter, a lion for St. Mark, a cross for Jesus Christ or Christianity, the chalice for Holy Communion, and a dove for the Holy Spirit.

For Christians, the sacraments are important because they are signs of God's grace or power. The water used in baptism symbolizes the cleansing power of God; the bread and wine in the Lord's Supper symbolize the spiritual nourishment we receive at the altar.

Some symbols, like hatchets and road signs, are *human* symbols. The crossed keys, lion, cross, chalice, and dove are also humanly chosen symbols which are helpful to us because they bring important ideas about our religion into our minds. But the water in baptism and the bread and wine in Holy Communion are divinely given symbols. They not only tell us something, or put an idea into our heads; they also *convey* something. The Church expresses this by saying that they are "effectual signs"; they do the very thing that they symbolize. So water, which symbolizes cleansing, does actually cleanse us from our sins when it is used in Holy Baptism. And bread and wine, which symbolize nourishment, do actually bring us the presence of Christ and strengthen us with His life when they are used in the Holy Communion.

184

Suggestions for further reading

The Hymnal: 20, 369 (stanza 1).
Other articles: Sacrament.

Questions

Your church no doubt has symbols in the building, on the altar, and on the minister's vestments. Can you "read" them? In Hymn 20 what does "Alpha and Omega" refer to? Think of five other symbols. What does each mean?

T

TEMPTATION
is the testing of our moral strength

ONCE A BOY saw a piece of paper blown from an open window by the wind. When he looked at it, he found it was a beautiful drawing of a ship in full sail. The idea came into his mind that he could trace this drawing and hand it in to the school paper as his own work. He had been trying to get a job on the paper as illustrator. This drawing was so good they would surely take him, and nobody would know it was not his own. His name would appear in print, which would make him feel fine. Also, he would work very hard to improve his drawing so the school paper would not suffer. In fact, he would actually be doing good —so how could it be wrong?

This was temptation. The boy was tempted to deceive, to *act a lie*. His case shows what is so often true: a temptation usually presents itself as something attractive and good. This is what makes it a test. If temptations were ugly or hard they would not tempt us. It would be easy to turn away and say "No!" It is their attractiveness that makes them tempting.

When Jesus was considering how He would carry on His ministry, He went through a time of testing. Afterward, He told His close friends that the real testings, or temptations, were to misuse the power God gave Him. To resist these attractive choices was a struggle—that is, He was actually tempted.

"But," you ask, "why does God let us be tempted?" Because through those struggles we can gain strength. If living a Christian life were easy, we would not grow. We would be soft and good for nothing. In this way, temptation is good.

God gives us freedom to make choices. He also gives us grace to resist temptation and to obey His will. But He doesn't interfere when we decide to go against His will.

There are stages in temptation: (1) the first suggestion; (2) the appeal of its attractiveness; (3) our choosing for or against. We cannot help being tempted, but if we pray to God, we *can* choose right. Only wrong *choosing* is sin. To avoid it, we need to ask God's help at once, acting as fast as we would to put out a fire.

When a temptation comes, and you find yourself being tested, do not resent it, or say, "This isn't fair!" Say rather, "Here it is! I am being tested. Help me, God, to resist and grow strong."

Suggestions for further reading

The Hymnal: 70.

Other articles: Conscience, Devil, Grace, Heaven, Hell, Sin.

Questions

What are some common temptations for you and your

friends? Why does the Lord's Prayer say, "Lead us not into temptation"? What has fasting during Lent to do with temptation?

TO TRESPASS
means to go against what is right

WHEN MEN GO FISHING or hunting, they have to watch for signs that read "No trespassing." These words mean they are not supposed to cross the line onto private or restricted property.

Perhaps you have a rule in your family about how late you can stay out at night. Your parents may say, "You may stay out, but not after nine-thirty. That is where we *draw the line*." If we step across a line or break a rule, we *transgress* or *trespass*.

In the Lord's Prayer, the word *trespass* means "transgression" or "debt." It means in part "to go against God's laws." God is love, and He wants our friendship and love. He wants to forgive us our trespasses so that we will be in the right relationship with Him, and He wants us to forgive others. He doesn't want us to be 50 per cent kind. You cannot be 75 per cent pure. And even if we were 100 per cent obedient today, it wouldn't make up for all our debt to God. Jesus says bluntly, "For if you forgive men their trespasses, your heavenly Father also will forgive you; but if you do not forgive men their trespasses, neither will your Father forgive your trespasses." (Matt. 6:14-15) Jesus told a parable about a servant who had a debt he could not pay, and so his master forgave him. Then the servant proceeded to collect debts from all who owed him, and he wouldn't forgive anyone. The master found out about it and insisted that the servant pay him after all. When the servant could not, the master had him punished.

Suggestions for further reading

The Hymnal: 361.
Other articles: Absolution, Forgiveness, Judgment, Reconciliation, Rejection, Sin, Temptation.

THE HOLY TRINITY
is God—the Father, the Son, and the Holy Spirit

THE WORD *trinity* means "three-ness," or "three-in-one." We know from the Bible that in the one God there are three Persons: Father, Son, and Holy Spirit (Holy Ghost). But God does not spend His time being first one Person of the Trinity and then another. He is always all three at once.

Also we know that these three Persons are related to one another in different ways. The Son comes from the Father, and the Holy Spirit comes from the Father through the Son. But this does not mean that the Son and the Holy Spirit are lower than the Father, or that first there was the Father and then, later, the Son and the Holy Spirit. All three Persons are equal; and the Son and the Holy Spirit, along with the Father, have had no beginning and will have no end.

Furthermore, each of the three Persons has a special relation to the world. In the Book of Common Prayer, on pages 284 and 285, we say:

"First, I learn to believe in God the Father, who hath made me, and all the world.

"Secondly, in God the Son, who hath redeemed me, and all mankind.

"Thirdly, in God the Holy Ghost, who sanctifieth me, and all the people of God."

Yet, although each of the three Persons has His special work, the other two Persons share it with Him. Divine Persons are different from human persons. They are stupendous. They are so knit together in Their infinite love for one another that They are actually one.

We cannot hope to understand this mystery fully. That would make us as great as God. There is nothing in heaven or earth to compare with God.

Here is a story about the great bishop St. Augustine. The bishop was walking one day on the seashore trying to figure out how God can be One and yet Three. Then he saw a child carrying water in a cup to a small hole dug in the sand. "What are you doing?" asked the bishop. The child replied, "I'm trying to pour the ocean into this hole." The bishop laughed and said, "That is impossible." The child looked up into St. Augustine's eyes and said, "It is no more impossible than for you to put Almighty God into your small mind." Then the child vanished.

Long before St. Augustine's time, the first disciples were puzzled. They were Jews, and they had known from infancy that there is only one God and that He is invisible. Yet they came to realize that their dear Friend and Master, Jesus, whom they had seen so often, was truly God. He told them, "I and the Father are one." (John 10:30) Yet on the other hand, He prayed again and again to the Father as to another person.

At last, on Pentecost, the Third Person came into the disciples' very hearts. "And they were all filled with the Holy Spirit and began to speak in other tongues, as the Spirit gave them utterance." (Acts 2:4.)

No wonder the disciples were puzzled. They knew there was only one God. But their experience of Jesus and the Holy Spirit gave them a bigger idea of God. Facts are facts, and the disciples would not deny them.

Think about these great matters as much as you like. Pray about them. Ask God to show you as much as is possible for a man to know about the Holy Trinity. But do not forget St. Augustine's vision of the child with the cup.

Glory be to the Father, and to the Son, and to the Holy Ghost; As it was in the beginning, is now, and ever shall be, world without end. Amen.

Suggestions for further reading

The Hymnal: 266, 268, 271.

Other articles: Atonement, Creation, God, Holy Spirit, Incarnation.

Questions

The triangle and three circles are common symbols for the Trinity. What do these symbols suggest to you about the Trinity? What are some other symbols of the Trinity?

What has God done for you as Father; as Son; as Holy Spirit?

U

UNCTION OF THE SICK
describes the Church's ministry of healing

JESUS TOLD HIS DISCIPLES to heal the sick. They often did this, anointing them with oil. (Mark 6:13) St. James says that if we are sick, we may ask the elders (priests) to anoint us. (Jas. 5:14–16) He advises us to confess our sins, and the Prayer Book gives that same advice in the rubrics on page 313. The reason is that if we have sins on our conscience and *keep them locked up* inside of us, they may make our sickness worse. The sensible thing is to make a clean breast and receive absolution. Then when the priest anoints us with oil or lays on his hands in blessing, our Lord's power can heal us, body and soul. (Prayer Book, page 320) We should also, of course, obey the doctor, because Unction is meant to bless his work, not to take its place.

Suggestions for further reading

The Hymnal: 515.

V

THE VIRGIN MARY

IN THE EPISCOPAL CHURCH in this country, over two hundred parishes are named for the Virgin Mary. She is mentioned eleven times in the Gospels for the feast days and Sundays given in the Book of Common Prayer, and we find her name in both the Apostles' and Nicene Creeds. We know her as the mother of Jesus who was born in Bethlehem, and we find her, after the Ascension, in prayer with the apostles and friends of Jesus Christ in the upper room in Jerusalem.

We often honor the mothers of great men in history. The mothers of George Washington and of Abraham Lincoln share in the favor we give to their sons. What is more natural than that the Church should honor the mother of Jesus Christ, our Saviour?

In the Gospel for the Annunciation we read: ". . . the angel Gabriel was sent from God unto a city of Galilee, named Nazareth, to a virgin espoused to a man whose name was Joseph, of the house of David; and the virgin's name was Mary. And the angel came in unto her, and said, Hail, thou that are highly favoured, the Lord is with thee: blessed art thou among women. And when she saw him, she was troubled at his saying, and cast in her mind what manner of salutation this should be. And the angel said unto her, Fear not, Mary: for thou hast found favour with God. And, behold, thou shalt conceive in thy womb, and bring forth a son, and shalt call his name JESUS. He shall be great, and shall be called the Son of the Highest: and the Lord God shall give unto him the throne of his father David: and he shall reign over the house of Jacob for ever; and of his kingdom there shall be no end. Then said Mary unto the angel, How shall this be, seeing I know not a man? And the angel answered and said unto her, The Holy Ghost shall come upon thee, and the power of the Highest shall overshadow thee: therefore also that holy thing which shall be born of thee shall be called the Son of God. . . . And Mary said, Behold the handmaid of the Lord; be it unto me according to thy word." (Page 236) This unquestioning obedience to the will of God made her the greatest human person ever to live.

Mary, in her humility, obedience, and faith, became, through the greatest miracle of all time, the mother of Jesus, who is God the Son incarnate. For this reason we give her all reverence short of what belongs to God alone.

Suggestions for further reading

The Hymnal: 17, 41, 117.

VOCATION
is God's call to you to be His friend and partner

IF YOU SAW JESUS, very busy and very tired with many people crowding around Him, and He beckoned to you and

194

asked you to do something for Him, what would you reply? But He *has* called you already! In fact He has called you twice.

First of all, He has called you to be His friend. You did not see Him beckon or hear His voice. But you can be sure that He wants *you* for He has made you different from all other living things. Plants and animals obey God, live their lives as God has planned, but only human beings can be His friends. Also, you are different from all other human beings. No one else is exactly like you. God has made you different in the hope that you will want to be His. He will not force you, of course, but He very much wants you. He is holding out His hand. This invitation to be His friend is your *vocation* as a Christian.

In the second place, God invites you to be His partner—to do the work for which He has given you gifts. You will be happy if you use the gifts He gave you. If you have the gifts to be a scientist, a doctor, an artist, or a farmer, that is the happy life for you. You will be happiest of all if you use your gifts and also dedicate them to the Friend who gave them to you—if you do your life work as a "thank you" to Him. The life work God has given specially to you is your *particular* vocation.

How can you find out what work God has for you? Don't expect to see a vision or hear a voice. Instead, do these four things:

1. *Pray*. If you want God to guide you, it's only common sense to ask Him.

2. *Think*. God's normal way of guiding you is to help you think clearly. Figure out as carefully as you can what opportunities you have, and what gifts.

3. *Take your time*. One of the surest signs that God is

guiding you is that, over a length of time, your prayers lead more and more to one conclusion.

4. *Make up your own mind.* Ask advice if you want to, but do not lean on your advisers or let them make your decisions. God wants *you* to choose.

Suggestions for further reading

The Hymnal: 408, 422, 506.

WHITSUNDAY
is the great Christian feast of the Holy Spirit

FIFTY DAYS AFTER our Lord had risen from the dead, the Holy Spirit came to his worshiping followers. This happened on an old Jewish feast day called Pentecost. The coming of the Spirit was the fulfillment of our Lord's promise, ". . . stay in the city, until you are clothed with power from on high." (Luke 24:49) That amazing experience is described in Acts 2:1–13. It was as if a mighty wind filled the room where the disciples were meeting. The faces of the men glowed with light like fire. Some outsiders even said the disciples were drunk. The Holy Ghost filled them with such joy and courage, they went out and proclaimed throughout the city that Jesus was Lord and Christ.

On this day the Church started to grow. It was possessed by a *new life* full of love and joy, power and hope. All shared the Spirit and were bound together by the Spirit's influence. The experience was so full of meaning for those who believed in the crucified and risen Lord that the Jewish feast of Pentecost became a great Christian festival equal to Easter and Christmas.

The meaning of this third, great high point of the Christian year is this: After Christ had ascended to heaven, the gift of God's Spirit to the faithful believers in the risen Lord bound them together in a faith-filled body which began to be a powerful influence on the lives of men and nations. Whitsunday, then, is the day on which we celebrate the awakening of the Christian Church to its God-given power and mission.

A possible explanation of the name *Whitsunday* is that it is a contraction of "White Sunday." Because of the climate in England, the eve of this day, rather than the eve of Easter, became the time for baptisms. It was called White Sunday from the white robes worn by those who were to be baptized.

Suggestions for further reading

The Hymnal: 108, 370.
Other articles: Christ, Holy Spirit, Mission, Pentecost.

Questions

We are familiar with the way our churches are decorated for Christmas and Easter. How would you suggest that we decorate for Whitsunday? What are the Christian symbols for the Holy Spirit? Why were they chosen?

A WITNESS
is one who tells the truth which he knows from his own experience concerning some person or event

THE TRUTH WHICH A WITNESS tells is called "evidence" or "testimony." For example, a witness in court takes an oath and promises to tell all he knows about something. Perhaps he saw an automobile accident and can say, "I was standing beside the road, and I saw a car come down the hill and then suddenly turn sharply to the left." As a witness, he gives information based on his own experience. He tells what he thinks he saw, what he believes is true.

The Greek word for witness is *martyr*. People who tell the truth at the cost of their lives are martyrs. In the very early days of Christianity there were followers of Jesus Christ who gave witness of their faith in our Lord by choosing to be killed rather than to deny Him or pretend that they were not Christians. This was giving or bearing witness by deeds as well as words.

A group of boys was about to go to the river for a swim. Just before they started, one of them beckoned to those who were standing nearest to him and said, "Hey! If we go around this side of the school and make it snappy, we can get rid of Tag-along. He's always in the way." So off they went like lightning. All, that is, except one boy who refused to enter into the trick. He went the other way, met Tag, and spent the rest of the afternoon with him, swimming in another place. Why? Because he wanted to make the unwanted boy feel that he was just as good as anybody. This was a case of bearing witness, because the boy showed a willingness to stand up for what he believed was right in spite of the objection of the group.

Everyone who stands up for Christ and His teachings is a witness for Him. As Peter said to Cornelius, the Roman officer, "And we are witnesses to all that he [Jesus] did. . . ." (Acts 10:39) Every missionary, therefore, is a witness. And every Christian should be a missionary, wherever he lives. When we are baptized, the minister says that the Church signs us with the sign of the Cross in token that we "shall not

be ashamed to confess the faith of Christ crucified, and man-
fully to fight under his banner . . ." To "confess the faith of
Christ crucified" is to stand up and be counted, publicly, as
a witness.

Suggestions for further reading

The Hymnal: 261, 423, 562.

Other articles: Acceptance, Confirmation, Fellowship,
Mission, Reconciliation.

Questions

What would you do about Tag-along? Have you ever
brought anyone new to church?

THE WORD OF GOD
means His self-revelation

WHEN YOU TALK TO SOMEBODY about an idea in your mind,
you have to use *words*. That is the way you make the idea
known to others. And the sum total of the words you use will
get your idea across so that the other person will understand.
(At least you hope so.) When we speak of the Word in
matters of Christian belief, we mean God's way of getting
Himself across. He tells us about Himself through His
Word.

In Christian thinking, Jesus Christ is called "The Word"
(as in John 1:1–14) because He is God's way of communi-
cating Himself to His human children. He is the Word
which "became flesh and dwelt among us." He is the way
God tells us about Himself. Of course Jesus Christ is not to
be separated from everything else that people have learned

about God. Other sources of God's self-revelation are sometimes called *words*.

The Bible is often called the Word of God, meaning the
message from God. It tells us how God prepared the Jewish
people for the coming of Christ; it tells us about the life of
Jesus in the days when He was visibly present with us, and
about the results of His coming. The Bible is God's testimony to us, especially in the stories about Jesus Christ; and
it brings God's Word home to our hearts and minds.

Suggestions for further reading

The Hymnal: 402.
Other articles: Bible, Gospel, Jesus.

TO WORSHIP GOD
is to give Him reverence and honor

WORSHIP ORIGINALLY MEANT "worthship." It is a way of
saying how much God is *worth* to the worshiper. Since
God's worth is beyond all measuring, it is impossible to give
Him too much reverence, honor, and obedience.

This may be true in theory, but unless I do something
about it, it means very little. Worship means that I make an
effort to show how important God really is. For example,
I might think it very important to be a sprinter and run one
hundred yards in ten seconds flat. But I have to practice and
keep in training if I am going to do it.

In this sense, if God is worth anything, we should worship Him in our work and play. People found out long ago
that we are not likely to do this unless we set aside times and
places in which to worship God in a special way. We do not

worship God *everywhere* unless we worship Him *some-where*. So the Church provides regular services of worship where we all come together as members of His family. God acts through the congregation to give us new power to obey Him. No one can be a Christian by himself, and public worship helps us to be unselfish in our prayers.

There are many kinds of public worship. Perhaps you are familiar with Morning Prayer. Think for a moment of what happens to you. You sing praises, hear the opening words, say the General Confession which is followed by the Declaration of Absolution, say the Lord's Prayer, respond with the versicles and sing the Venite, read a psalm, hear the lessons and respond with canticles, say the Creed, hear and join in the prayers, sing a hymn, hear a sermon, give your offering, hear the Blessing, and sing another hymn.

The central act of worship in the Church is Holy Communion. We hear the commandments and two passages from the Bible, say the Creed, pray for all men, confess our sins and hear the Absolution, then we offer ourselves and participate in the great prayers leading to the act of communion. After this come the Thanksgiving and Blessing.

In addition to Morning Prayer and Holy Communion, our Prayer Book gives us the order for Evening Prayer, the Litany, and services for many special occasions. People are baptized, confirmed, and married in church. Finally, they are taken to the church for the burial office. All these services help us to remember that God stands at the center of our lives and of the universe.

Sometimes we sing:

"Like a might army
Moves the Church of God . . ." (Hymn 557)

If you were in the United States Army, and the sergeant asked where you were at parade time, what would happen if your buddy said, "Joe was out late last night and was too tired to get up this morning"? Would the sergeant say he was so sorry you couldn't be present to hear the music of the band?

The Church isn't "like a mighty army" when one of us tells the rector, "I wasn't there last Sunday because it was the last chance to get my model airplanes ready for the Hobby Show," or "It was the first time this winter the skating has been good"! If the Church is going to be "like a mighty army," we had better be in the congregation each Sunday.

Suggestions for further reading

The Hymnal: 398, 557.

The Book of Common Prayer: The series of services for special occasions beginning on page 273.

Other articles: Absolution, Canticle, Church, Creed, Holy Communion, Prayer, Sunday.

Questions

Members of some communions are supposed to go to church every Sunday. What are we supposed to do? (See the Prayer Book, page 291.) Why do we call our Prayer Book the Book of *Common* Prayer?

CROSS-REFERENCE INDEX

THE TREATMENT OF THE WORDS IN THIS BOOK is not intended to be exhaustive but instead to arouse the interest of young people and their teachers. Those who want to read further on the subjects covered are referred to the six volumes of THE CHURCH'S TEACHING. In the cross-reference index which follows, letters refer to individual volumes (as indicated in the key below) and numbers to the pages involved.

206

208

SUGGESTIONS FOR BIBLE STUDY

THE FOLLOWING BIBLE REFERENCES are given in addition to those mentioned in the text. The purpose of this list is to provide material that will lead the reader to a deeper appreciation of the words as they are used, or implied, in their Biblical setting. It is suggested that you use these passages for meditation and study, rather than for lesson material.

The list is by no means all-inclusive. In some cases it may not give the references that seem most obvious to you. It is hoped it will do a greater service by enriching your background than by merely confirming what you already know.

Absolution	Luke 5:17–26; John 20:19–23
Acceptance	Gen. 45:1–5; Mark 10:13–16; Luke 19: 1–10; 23:33–43
Adultery	II Sam. 11:1–12:10; Matt. 5:27–32; John 8:1–11
Advent	John 1:19–28; Phil. 4:4–7
Almighty	Luke 23:32–34; Rom. 8:31–39; Rev. 4

Kingdom of God	Luke 10:1–24; 11:1–20 (See also "Parable.")
Law	Exod. 19:1–8; Deut. 8:1–6; Ps. 119:33–48 Rom. 13:8–10; I Cor. 10:23–33
Love	Hos. 11:1–9; Luke 15:11–32; Rom. 13 8–10; I John 4:7–21
Holy Matrimony	See the Epistle and Gospel for a Marriage Prayer Book, pp. 267–268.
Mediator	II Cor. 5:11–20; Eph. 2:11–22
Mission	Matt. 28:16–20; John 10:1–18; Acts 28 23–31; Gal. 2:1–10
Murder	Exod. 20:13; 21:12–15; Matt. 5:21–26 Rom. 12:17–21; 13:8–10
Name	Acts 3:1–4:12; Phil. 2:5–11
Obey	Jer. 11:1–8; Dan. 3:1–30
Parable	Mark 4:1–34; 13
Passion	Matt. 26:36–27:54; Mark 14:32–15:39 Luke 22:39–23:49; John 18:1–20:37
Penitence	Job 42:1–6; Pss. 32; 38; Isa. 57:14–15; Jer 14:7–9
Prayer	Jer. 14:7–9; Matt. 6:5–15; Luke 11:1–13 Jas. 5:13–16
Reconciliation	Rom. 5:1–11; Col. 1:9–23
Redemption	Job 19:23–27; Ps. 130; Isa. 43:1–7; Luke 1 68–79; Rom. 3:21–30
Rejection	Ps. 22:1–19; Mark 10:13–16; 14:3–9; 14:43 –15:37
Repentance	Ps. 51; Jer. 3:11–15
Resurrection	I Cor. 15
Right	Pss. 19:7–14; 119:97–112

Sacrifice	Ps. 4; Rom. 5:1–11; 12:1–3
Saint	Eph. 4:1–13
Salvation	Pss. 18:1–3; 118; Luke 1:46–57
Sanctify	John 17; Heb. 2
Saviour	Matt. 11:2–6; John 4:1–42; Acts 13:13–42
Second Coming	Matt. 25:31–46; Luke 21:25–36
Secure	Pss. 27; 91; Matt. 7:16–29
Separation	Matt. 26:69–75; Mark 14:1–21
Sin	Isa. 1:1–20; Jer. 7:21–28; Rom. 7:7–25
Soul and Spirit	Ezek. 37:1–14; I Cor. 2:10–13
Steal	Rom. 2:17–29
Steward	Luke 12:42–48; 17:7–10; I Cor. 4:1–5; I Pet. 4:10–11
Temptation	Matt. 4:1–11; Luke 22:24–34; I Cor. 10:1–13
Trespass	Mark 11:24–26
Trinity	Eph. 4:4–6; Rev. 1:4–6
Unction of the Sick	Mark 5:21–24, 35–43
Vocation	Exod. 3:1–15; Jer. 1:4–10; Acts 9:1–18
Whitsunday	Acts 2:1–11
Witness	Acts 1:6–9; 4:5–20; 5:17–39; I John 1:1–4
Word of God	Rom. 10:1–13; Col. 3:12–17
Worship	Pss. 95; 96; 99; Isa. 44:6–23

HOW THIS BOOK WAS REVISED

THIS IS A REVISED EDITION of *More Than Words*, originally published in 1955. The work of revision was done by a committee of the following five people:

THE REV. W. NORMAN PITTENGER, S.T.D., Professor of Christian Apologetics, The General Theological Seminary.

MISS ELEANOR E. SANDT, M.A., Junior-High-School Editor, Division of Curriculum Development, Department of Christian Education.

THE REV. CHARLES W. F. SMITH, D.D., Professor of New Testament, Episcopal Theological School.

THE REV. WILLIAM SYDNOR, M.A., Executive Secretary, Division of Curriculum Development, Department of Christian Education.

A representative of the Order of the Holy Cross, the REV. WILLIAM R. D. TURKINGTON, present Father Superior of the Order, attended the early meetings of the committee, and the REV. JOHN S. BALDWIN, O.H.C., represented the Order at the final meeting.

216